The Prophetic Mandate

Books by Chip Brogden

Strength for the Journey
Why Do You Call Me Lord?
Infinite Supply
The Ekklesia
The Irresistible Kingdom
The Irresistible Life
Getting Babylon Out of You
Embrace the Cross
The Church in the Wilderness
Lord of All
Simple Truth

THE PROPHETIC MANDATE

*Declaring the Purposes
of God in the End-Times*

CHIP BROGDEN

The Prophetic Mandate:
Declaring the Purposes of God in the End-Times

©2013 Chip Brogden

Published by The School of Christ
http://www.TheSchoolOfChrist.Org

Contents

Preface

This is one of the most urgently needed books I have ever written. *If we don't learn how to recognize, restore, and receive from the genuinely prophetic men and women in the Body of Christ then the purity and simplicity of a Christ-Centered Faith will be lost.*

If you think I'm overstating the problem then you don't fully appreciate the danger of our times.

The purpose of all prophetic speaking is *to reveal Christ* – to bring Him more clearly into view. Those inspired to speak or proclaim something by the Holy Spirit should be helping to direct our attention onto Christ and away from everything that distracts us. The prophetic voice should rise up like a trumpet to bring clarity and direction out of confusion and misunderstanding. It is not just truth stated in an inspirational way, it is *the truth concerning Jesus* spoken by those who know Him and can lead others to Him.

But of all things, the "prophetic ministry" today does more to distract us from Jesus than to tell us the truth concerning Jesus. In fact, it is difficult to find Jesus at all in most of what is touted today as "prophetic."

So what is the prophetic ministry as God *intends* it to be? What is a prophet? What do prophets do? Do they have a place in our generation? If so, what?

To answer these questions, we begin with a thorough examination of the prophetic ministry to determine whether or not it is valid for us today; then, what the prophetic ministry is not, what it is, and some general and specific requirements of prophets.

From there, we explore the hidden work of prayer, fasting, and ministering to the Lord as fundamental functions of the prophetic calling to give the reader a better sense for the depth of relationship required of someone called to this particular role.

Finally, we look at the responsibility of the prophetic ministry to safeguard and uphold the Testimony of Jesus in the Earth. We conclude with some sobering warnings of what we can expect in days to come, as well as some positive steps we can take right now to better prepare God's people for spiritual conflict in the Last Days.

These ideas may seem far removed from the popular concept of what the prophetic ministry is. They certainly seem disconnected from what is commonly accepted (and what passes for) "prophetic ministry." I hope to elevate the discussion beyond the subjective, personal realm and provide a perspective that can only be obtained by rising above what is popular and common in order to embrace what is *true*.

This book is dedicated to the restoration and encouragement of the Christ-centered, Spirit-led prophetic calling to ensure that the next generation will still have a pure testimony of the truth concerning Jesus.

Chip Brogden
Canandaigua, N.Y.
November, 2012

Chapter One

Are Prophets For Today?

"The Lord God does nothing without revealing His secret to His servants the prophets" (Amos 3:7).

D o prophets still exist? Is the prophetic ministry for today, or does the prophetic ministry belong to a time gone by? Do we still need prophets to speak the words of God to us? Don't the Scriptures that we already have suffice? Do we not have the Holy Spirit as our Teacher and Guide, the Revealer of all Truth? Is this sufficient, or does God still find it necessary to use men and women in a prophetic manner? If so, why?

Let us look at the issue of the prophetic ministry and its relevance for our time. Scripture establishes what has come to be known as "the five-fold ministry" as a foundation for the Ekklesia. This is a spiritual leadership made up of five types of people, each with their own particular function. They are: apostles, prophets, evangelists, pastors and teachers.

"And He Himself gave some to be **apostles**, some **prophets**, some **evangelists**, and some **pastors** and **teachers**, for the equipping of the saints for the work of ministry, for the edifying of the body of Christ, till we all come to the unity of the faith and of the knowledge of the Son of God, to a perfect man, to the measure of the stature of the fullness of Christ; that we should no longer be children, tossed to and fro and carried about with every wind of doctrine, by the trickery of men, in the cunning craftiness of deceitful plotting, but, speaking the truth in love, may grow up in all things into Him who is the head—Christ—from whom the whole body, joined and knit together by what every joint supplies, according to the effective working by which every part does its share, causes growth of the body for the edifying of itself in love" (Eph. 4:11-16).

Since the prophet is included together with apostles, evangelists, pastors, and teachers, we would do well to ask: Are apostles for today? Are evangelists for today? Are pastors for today? Are teachers for today? There is no Scriptural basis for teaching that some (like evangelists, pastors, and teachers) are for today, yet others (like apostles and prophets) are no longer needed. We can accept them all, or we can discard them all, but we cannot pick and choose those we want to keep and those we want to be rid of.

So the real question is: Are any of these ministry gifts still needed today? Do we still need apostles? Do we still need prophets? Do we still need evangelists? Do we still need pastors? Do we still need teachers?

To answer this, let us take a step back and look at the five-fold ministry gifts; not individually, but as a whole. Who are they? They are people, first and foremost. These are not "offices" or "positions." We must not look at this with an institutional mindset the way we would look at a business organization chart.

The Ekklesia is the Family of God (Eph. 3:15). Within this Family are many brothers and sisters. Some are older, some are younger. In a healthy family, the older naturally serve, protect, care for, and watch over the younger.

Since the Ekklesia is the Family of God, it stands to reason that God would give responsibility to certain older, more mature brothers and sisters to help the younger brothers and sisters. Thus, Scripture declares that it is God Who gave "some" until "all" have come to maturity. These "some" are considered *elders* simply because they are *older*, i.e., *more mature spiritually*. These elders were not elected officials, office holders, or religious bureaucrats. God simply said that the older members of the Ekklesia are responsible for helping the younger members.

The word "for" answers the question of what these ministry gifts are supposed to do; they are here *for* three things: 1) for the perfection of the saints; 2) for the work of the ministry; 3) for the edification of the Body of Christ. God desires that brothers and sisters in the Ekklesia help one another. The older must watch over the younger, and the younger must allow themselves to be helped by the older and more experienced: "Likewise you younger people, submit yourselves to your elders. Yes, all of you be submissive to one another" (1 Pet. 5:5a).

God might have declared that the Holy Spirit and the Scriptures were sufficient guidance, and that no human interaction was needed or necessary. Given the abuses of carnal people in positions of religious power, we might wonder why God did not bypass the man or woman altogether and always lead us directly. Indeed, He could have easily done so; but He did not do so. Instead, He established the Ekklesia as a Family, with the intent that we would grow together, helping one another.

How long is the five-fold ministry supposed to endure? Are these functions intended to last forever, or are they scheduled to expire at some point? The answer is: there is a definite duration during which these ministries will remain in force. The key word is "until." So they are only for a season. Certain conditions must be fulfilled, and once they are fulfilled, they will no longer be needed. What are these conditions? There are four requirements associated with the word *until*:

1. Until we all come in the unity of the faith;
2. Until we all have the full-knowledge of the Son of God;
3. Until we are all fully grown, no longer children;
4. Until we all have attained the measure of the stature of the fullness of Christ.

It is now fairly simple to determine the relevance of these ministries today. Prayerfully consider these seven questions:

1. Have the saints been perfected?
2. Has the work of the ministry been completed?
3. Does the Body of Christ still need to be edified?
4. Have we all come into the unity of the faith?

5. Do we all have the full-knowledge of the Son of God?
6. Have we all become full-grown and spiritually mature?
7. Have we all attained to the measure of the stature of the fullness of Christ?

It should be apparent that while this may describe "few" or "some" it can by no means apply to "all." Not yet, anyway.

We conclude, therefore, that the five-fold ministries are not only applicable and relevant for the Ekklesia today, they are desperately and urgently needed. To the extent that we fail to recognize, acknowledge, support, and receive from the very ones given by God to help the Ekklesia grow into spiritual maturity, to that same extent we will suffer from spiritual immaturity.

The next key word is "that." This will answer all questions concerning "why." Why did God give these ministry gifts to the Ekklesia? Why are they so critically important? And why should we be willing to recognize and receive from them? The answer:

> "That we should no longer be children, tossed to and fro and carried about with every wind of doctrine, by the trickery of men, in the cunning craftiness of deceitful plotting, but, speaking the truth in love, may grow up in all things into Him who is the head—Christ—from whom the whole body, joined and knit together by what every joint supplies, according to the effective working by which every part does its share, causes growth of

the body for the edifying of itself in love." (Eph. 4:14-16).

Without the older brothers and sisters to watch over them, the younger brothers and sisters will be tossed to and fro, blown around by different teachings, deceived and led astray from the simplicity of Christ. Children are innocent and naïve, and therefore easily misled, abused, deceived and taken advantage of. They don't appreciate the dangers of wandering into the street, swallowing unknown substances, or talking to strangers. They need adult supervision. Likewise, spiritual children haven't yet learned how to exercise discernment. They are unfamiliar and inexperienced in the ways of the Lord. You tell them that they should just follow the Holy Spirit, but they don't yet know how. You tell them they should just read the Bible, but they aren't familiar with the written Word of God and they don't know what to do with it. Jesus didn't tell His disciples to "go look it up." He taught them. He helped them.

Spiritual children have only just begun their journey. In addition to the Holy Spirit and the Scriptures, they need the wisdom of older brothers and sisters to help them along the path to spiritual maturity. Once they are "fully grown" they can then return the favor by watching over and helping the ones coming up behind them. This is the will of God for our spiritual growth and maturity.

Are there exceptions? Could God raise someone from spiritual infancy to spiritual adulthood without any help from older brothers and sisters? With God, anything is possible; but that doesn't mean everything is permissible. He gave "some" to the Ekklesia for good reason, and there is no indication that He ever took them back again, or provided for an alternative means of raising spiritual children. The Ethiopian eunuch summed it up nicely in his frustrated reply to Philip: "How can I understand unless someone explains it to me?" (Acts 8:31). Paul echoed this sentiment:

> "How can they call on Him to save them unless they believe in Him? And how can they believe in Him if they have never heard about Him? And how can they hear about Him unless someone tells them?" (Rom. 10:14, NLT).

If we accept God's description of the Ekklesia as the Family of God, and we recognize that the five-fold ministries are still needed, then we have the answers to our original questions concerning the prophetic ministry. Yes, prophets are for today. Yes, we still need prophetic men and women, along with other older and gifted believers in the Ekklesia, to help all come to spiritual maturity.

This opens the door to a new range of things to be considered. If prophets exist, and prophets are needed and necessary today, who are they? Where are they? What are they supposed to be doing? What does the prophetic ministry look like now?

Four Misconceptions About the Prophetic Ministry

> "Thus says the Lord God: 'Woe to the foolish prophets, who follow their own spirit and have seen nothing!'" (Eze. 13:3).

If we accept the fact that prophets exist and are needed today, does it follow that we should simply accept all who claim to be "prophetic" and receive whatever they declare? That would be a mistake. For just as we should be careful to avoid false teachers, we must also exercise caution and avoid false prophets. Jesus gave several warnings concerning false prophets:

> "Beware of false prophets, who come to you in sheep's clothing, but inwardly they are ravenous wolves... many false prophets will rise up and deceive many... for false christs and false prophets will rise and show great signs and wonders to deceive, if possible, even the elect." (Mt. 7:15; 24:11,24).

Genuine prophets were an integral part of the early Ekklesia, but along with the authentic prophetic calling, there were also false prophets to be on guard against:

> "Beloved, do not believe every spirit, but test the spirits, whether they are of God; because many false prophets have gone out into the world" (1 Jn. 4:1).

The abundance of immature, misguided, or outright deceptive false prophetic expressions today has contributed to a great deal of misunderstanding and confusion concerning the prophetic ministry. This should come as no surprise. The prophetic voice is critical to God's Kingdom and Purpose. The prophet is a vital element that contributes to the spiritual growth of the Ekklesia. For those very reasons, the prophetic man or woman attracts the attention of our spiritual adversary, who is keenly interested in quenching, distorting, counterfeiting, and silencing any genuine prophetic expression in the earth. So long as the prophetic voice is prevented, the spiritual growth and maturity of the Ekklesia is hindered, and the ultimate purposes of God remain unfulfilled and unrealized. Flooding the land with a multitude of false witnesses is one of the enemy's favorite and most common methods of drowning out the genuinely prophetic man or woman.

To discern the genuine, we must learn to recognize and ignore the false. The easiest way to do this is to first say what the prophetic gift *is not*. Then we can more clearly see what it is.

In my experience, there are four popular misconceptions of what constitutes something as prophetic. We have tested this in the real world and proven it time and time again. All we have to do is announce a prophetic conference (I've conducted a few) and it is almost guaranteed to attract representatives of all four schools of confused thought about what makes something "prophetic," each arriving with their own expectation of what they will find.

Misconception #1 – The Prophetic means "End Times"

Eschatology is the Biblical study of the last days, or end times events. Because the prophets in the Scriptures frequently prophesied about events that would happen towards the end of the world, it is easy for the uninformed to assume that "prophetic" simply means anything to do with the "last days" or "end times." If something has a predictive element to it, they think it must be "prophetic." Favorite topics include the Rapture, the Antichrist, the Mark of the Beast, the Tribulation, the Book of Revelation, and so forth.

It is all very fascinating and interesting to interpret current events through the lens of Biblical prophecy, but eschatology does not rise to the level of being described as "prophetic" in the sense that Ephesians 4 describes the prophetic gift. That is to say, studying end time events or listening to eschatological prophecy teachers simply does not go very far towards producing spiritually mature believers in Jesus. When these folks attend my prophetic conferences they feel the weekend was wasted if I did not teach from the Book of Revelation and talk about 666. That's just where they are at.

Misconception #2 – The Prophetic means "Spiritual Warfare"

Many teachings on spiritual warfare have evolved out of the Charismatic movement. These teachings typically describe things such as strategic-level intercession, spiritual mapping, pulling down strongholds, naming territorial spirits, Jericho marches, and other acts that are supposed to have some effect on the spirits of darkness. While spiritual warfare is a Biblical concept, there is little Scriptural basis for these particular practices; instead, the teachings rely heavily on anecdotal "evidence" for support. They did something once, it seemed to work, so now it is part of their spiritual warfare manual. This is cause enough for concern; but once these practices are described as "prophetic" and the leaders are considered "prophets" then those who know the ways of God more accurately must point out that the prophetic calling has little to do with battling territorial spirits – at least not in the manner previously described.

The true prophet does not battle for spiritual victory, but declares a victory that has already been seen, experienced, and entered into. This disqualifies most spiritual warfare methodology as too carnal and fleshly to be considered prophetic. When these folks attend my prophetic conferences they wonder why I don't bind the devil, cast down strongholds, and rebuke all the territorial spirits over the city, county, state, nation, and continent we're meeting in. After all, how can it be prophetic if it doesn't fight the devil? They are deeply entrenched in this mindset and it is difficult to move them from it.

Misconception #3 – The Prophetic means "Personal Prophecy"

Far too many only think of the prophetic ministry in terms of personal words of prophecy. They constantly seek a "thus saith the Lord" type of message from someone to give them instant encouragement, personal guidance, or specific direction. On the one hand, God certainly does use prophetic people to speak words of encouragement and direction to us from time to time. On the other hand, God does not tell us to *seek these messages out*, or to rely on them as our sole means of guidance. The reason is simple: God wishes for us to know Him, to learn His ways, to search His Word, and to learn to hear from Him directly for ourselves. The prophetic word, when and if it comes to us through other people, should ideally bring confirmation of what the Lord has already shown us. There are two kinds of people in this category who attend my prophetic conferences: those looking to *receive* a personal word of prophecy, and those looking to *give* one. The former is drawn to the latter like a moth is drawn to the flame – and the end result is that eventually somebody usually gets burned.

This situation can be avoided if we accept the fact that the prophetic ministry is supposed to help you become spiritually mature; it is not intended to micromanage your every move and take the place of the Holy Spirit in your life. We must also learn the difference between the prophetic calling of Ephesians 4 and the simple gift of prophecy in 1 Corinthians 14. All *may* prophesy; but not all who prophesy are called to the prophetic ministry. However, in my prophetic conferences, no matter how much God says through the teaching, these people will go home saddened if I don't wave my hand over them and give them a "thus saith the Lord" kind of personal prophecy.

Misconception #4 – The Prophetic means "Big Revival"

Yet another stream of prophetic misunderstanding has arisen out of the belief that God wishes to pour out His Spirit in one last "big revival" that will shake the earth and bring in a final harvest of souls before the end of the age. Adherents typically combine all three prophetic misconceptions – eschatology, spiritual warfare, and personal prophecy – into one big movement of people who always see God getting ready to "do something." I hope they are right; but right or wrong, none of this rises to the level of being prophetic. At best, we might call it evangelistic. Many evangelists, not content with being evangelists, try to cast themselves as prophets in order to attract greater attention. But they are clearly evangelists, and have no business describing themselves (or allowing themselves to be described) as apostles or prophets. If they attend my prophetic conferences, they will be disappointed if I don't gather everybody around the front to weep and cry until they feel the power of God "move" on them.

* * * *

If none of the things we commonly accept as "prophetic" are actually prophetic, what does *prophetic* mean, and what *is* a prophet?

Chapter Two

What is a Prophet?

*"God, who at various times and in various ways spoke
in time past to the fathers by the prophets, has in these
last days spoken to us by His Son... The testimony of
Jesus is the spirit of prophecy" (Heb. 1:1,2a; Rev.
19:10b).*

A prophet (in the best Biblical sense of the word) is
*a person who discerns and declares, by the
inspiration of the Holy Spirit, the purposes of God
concerning Christ.* We will develop that thought and
build support for it as we progress.

Because of the popular misconceptions of the
prophetic ministry, some may initially find this
definition too narrow. They may struggle with the idea
that all prophetic utterance is Christ-centered. For
instance, what about all those end time events in the
Book of Revelation? Some of them do not seem to
directly speak about Jesus. Are they not prophetic?

This objection is easily overcome, but before we can
overcome it, we must recognize one supreme, central,
eternal truth: that *everything God has done, is doing,
and will do is connected somehow to bringing Christ
more fully into view.* Everything that God has said, is
saying, and will say (prophetically or otherwise) is

related to Christ: either directly, or indirectly, it all points and leads to Him. We can safely discard as "interesting, but not prophetic" anything that *claims* to be prophetic but does not reveal or declare something concerning Christ.

The Book of Revelation does not contradict our narrow definition; it supports it. Indeed, the first verse of the Book of Revelation confirms that the entire writing is "the revelation *of Jesus Christ*." Christ is indeed revealed in the midst of the Ekklesia with awesome titles that include "Ruler of the Kings of the Earth" (one of my personal favorites)... Faithful Witness... Firstborn from the Dead... The Lord God... The Almighty... King of Kings... Lord of Lords... Faithful and True... The Lamb... The Lion... The Root and Offspring of David... He Who Was, And Is, and Is To Come... the Alpha and Omega, the Beginning and End, the First and Last..." and so on. Christ is the Subject of the Book.

So while The Book of Revelation says a great deal about the end of the world, that is not what makes it *prophetic.* Its true prophetic purpose is not to reveal things happening in the last days, but to reveal the *preeminence and victory of Christ* in the last days. John gives us the Key there in the very first verse, and with this Key you can unlock the meaning behind all that is revealed in the Book of Revelation. Christ is the Key. Without this Key, all attempts to interpret and understand the Book of Revelation are futile.

So the Book of Revelation not only reveals Christ, it reveals that Christ is the purpose and intention of all Spirit-inspired prophetic utterance:

> "The testimony of Jesus is the spirit of prophecy" (Rev. 19:10b).

Here are some other translations of Revelation 19:10b that are worth looking at:

> "The essence of prophecy is to give a clear witness for Jesus" (NLT).

> "The substance (essence) of the truth revealed by Jesus is the spirit of all prophecy (the vital breath, the inspiration of all inspired preaching and interpretation of the divine will and purpose, including both mine and yours" (AMP).

The Amplified is good, but it gives the impression that prophecy is general "truth" that Jesus reveals. This is incorrect. It is not truth revealed *by* Jesus; it is the truth *concerning* Jesus. Jesus is the Subject of prophecy. *Christ Himself* is the purpose of all prophetic revelation and declaration. Knox is the most accurate:

> "It is the truth concerning Jesus which inspires all prophecy" (Knox).

"The truth concerning Jesus" is a fair translation of "The Testimony of Jesus." The prophetic ministry is zealous for the *truth* concerning Jesus, and it finds itself opposed to all *falsehood* concerning Jesus. This is the foundation of all prophetic ministry and the basis of all spiritual conflict, since the spirit of Antichrist obviously has the exact opposite goal.

We will have more to say about the Testimony of Jesus in due course. For now, it is enough if we simply settle upon this one principle forever: *the prophetic word (and therefore, the prophetic ministry and the prophetically gifted person) has always been, is, and forever will be, the primary means through which the truth concerning Jesus (The Testimony) is revealed and declared to the world.*

If that seems far-fetched, take a step back from the Book of Revelation, and look at the entire Bible. Where did it come from? How did it get here? Why has it persisted against all efforts to destroy it? It has endured because the Bible is a prophetic book, written by prophetic people who were inspired by the Holy Spirit to prophetically declare the Truth concerning Jesus: either openly, in parable, in proverb, or in prophecy. Christ is the central theme of God's eternal Purpose, and so He must, of course, be the Subject of God's written revelation to man. Jesus declared that "the Scriptures testify of Me" (Jn. 5:39). And so they do. Those who know how to rightly divide the Written Word can find Christ the Living Word in every book, in every chapter. Some revelations of Christ are in plain sight. For example, Jesus is easily seen and met in Matthew, Mark, Luke, and John. The Old Testament prophets declare Him in types and shadows, while the rest of the New Testament declares Him more clearly in this age and in the age to come.

From Genesis to Revelation, the Bible contains the revelation of Christ. It is the Testimony of Jesus in written form. How the Spirit of Antichrist has tried to destroy this written Testimony of Jesus! All attempts to destroy this Book have failed. Today, the preferred method of the enemy is not to destroy the Book, but to get us to destroy ourselves by ignoring the Book. This has worked remarkably well. "My people are destroyed for lack of knowledge" (Hos. 4:6a).

The fact that we can casually accept so many words, visions, dreams, teachings, and experiences as "prophetic" when they do not reveal *the truth concerning Jesus* reflects the lack of knowledge that this book seeks to correct. Prophetic utterance does not deal with "things," but with Christ. When the prophetic revelation is genuine, we will be able to answer the question: "What about *this* tells me something about *Christ*?" If we cannot find something of Christ in it, then whatever it is, it isn't prophetic. May God show us the difference.

Qualifications of the Prophet

There are two layers of qualification for a prophet today. The prophet must first meet the general requirements of anyone in the five-fold ministry. Once that has been satisfied, the prophet must then meet the specific requirements of his or her unique function as a prophet.

General Requirements to Be Met

We have already established that the prophetic person is part of the five-fold ministry given by God to help the Ekklesia come to spiritual maturity in Christ. This brings the prophetic ministry under a single umbrella that covers all the ministry gifts. This is the framework that governs (or should govern) all ministry in the Ekklesia. This means that while there are differences in function and gift, the fundamental purpose of each person in the five-fold ministry is the same.

We cannot lead others spiritually to a place that we have not already seen and entered into. We can therefore conclude that if "some" are given in order to help "all" reach a certain place in the Lord, those "some" have already reached that place. Otherwise, how could they possibly guide others into the same place?

So, based on our reading, we see four goals for the Ekklesia. We simply take the four goals for the "all" and translate them into four requirements for the "some" in the five-fold ministry. To serve others, they must first be...

1. *Spiritually mature.* They must be elder
   (older) members of the Ekklesia. That
   means they have walked with the Lord, and
   are experienced in His ways. They are not
   new believers. They are not babes, still
   drinking milk. They can eat meat, and they
   can feed meat to others. Spiritual maturity
   does not mean sinless perfection; it simply
   means one is old enough to no longer be
   considered a child. Older brothers and
   sisters are not beyond reproach or rebuke
   when they sin; on the contrary, they are to
   be corrected publicly as an example to the
   rest (1 Tim. 5:20). But the general idea is
   that, having walked with the Lord for a
   longer period of time, they are thus more
   conformed to the image of Christ, setting
   the example of purity and holiness.

2. *Able to edify the Ekklesia.* Babies, children,
   teenagers, even young adults are primarily
   concerned with getting their own needs
   met. But when you become a parent,
   everything changes. You realize you are
   responsible for taking care of your children.
   You now have a purpose bigger than
   supporting yourself. You will sacrifice
   anything so long as your children are cared
   for. Similarly, spiritually mature adults
   have moved beyond getting their own
   needs met and are now concerned with

meeting the needs of others. This is the primary indicator that they have actually crossed the threshold into spiritual adulthood. They are givers, not takers; providers, not consumers. They are true "elders" in the sense that they are willing to watch over, serve, protect, and provide for the "youngers."

3. *Unified in The Faith.* What is the *unity of the Faith*? It cannot mean that we all agree on every doctrinal nuance; instead, it means that we discard non-essential doctrinal nuance in favor of a Christ-centered Faith. Older brothers and sisters have learned the hard way that only One Thing is needed (Lk. 10:42). One of the primary duties of the older is to help the younger learn that not every battle is worth fighting. Foolish arguments and peripheral issues irrelevant to God's ultimate purposes can be set aside. This is a mark of spiritual maturity and a basic qualification for ministry in the Ekklesia. It is the first step towards unifying us in a Christ-centered faith.

4. *Christ-Centered.* God's goal for the Ekklesia is not a self-centered faith, not a church-centered faith, but a Christ-Centered Faith: a faith where Christ is

preeminent, ruling and reigning – not in a theoretical, theological sense, but in a real and practical sense. It is easy to be distracted by many things that come to take our eyes off of Christ. When this occurs we stop growing spiritually. In order to keep the Ekklesia on the narrow path towards spiritual maturity, older brothers and sisters must have already come to "the knowledge (*Greek: epignosis – full-knowledge, experiential knowledge*) of the Son of God." They must have already seen the danger of getting their eyes off of Christ and have learned how to stay focused on Him: how to be Christ-centered. How will they protect, preserve, and proclaim a Christ-centered faith if they are not living a Christ-centered life themselves? To be fully submitted to His Lordship is to arrive at "the measure of the stature of the fullness of Christ" – spiritual maturity.

We can and should apply these general qualifications to anyone who claims to be an apostle, evangelist, pastor, or teacher. If they are not leading people down a path towards Christ-centered spiritual maturity then they have failed their most basic purpose and are disqualified. No further inquiry is necessary. If they are not too far gone then perhaps they can be restored, but as long as the general requirements go lacking, they are Scripturally unqualified for anything related to the five-fold ministry. Note how many unqualified people nevertheless assume the title and position of a function for which they are ill-suited and ill-prepared. We should pay careful attention to what Scripture requires and prevent further damage to the Body of Christ.

In the previous examples provided under "prophetic misconceptions" it is easy to disqualify what is commonly labeled as "prophetic" simply because they each fail to pass the general requirements of all five-fold ministry gifts. We do not even have to examine the special requirements in those cases because the general requirements are not met. For example, none of the examples previously cited contribute to the Christ-centered spiritual growth and maturity of the Ekklesia; quite the opposite, in fact. Not only do people with those misconceptions fail to grow spiritually, they are very easily "tossed to and fro" with strange teachings and unbiblical practices. Since this runs contrary to the very purpose for which the five-fold ministry gifts were given by God, it demonstrates that (whatever it is) it is not *prophetic*.

Three Specific Requirements for Prophets

Once the general requirements of the five-fold ministry are fulfilled, we can then look into each of the ministries individually and determine the specific requirements for each. In this book we are primarily concerned with the prophetic ministry. So what is its purpose? How does it uniquely contribute to the

Christ-centered spiritual growth and spiritual maturity of the Ekklesia?

Recall our working definition: *a prophet is a person who discerns and declares, by the inspiration of the Holy Spirit, the purposes of God concerning Christ*. To be able to do this consistently and effectively, three distinctive things are required of the prophet.

Prophetic Requirement #1 – Wholly Governed by the Holy Spirit

The purpose of the prophetic ministry is to reveal Christ. The purpose of the Holy Spirit is to reveal Christ. Thus, the Holy Spirit and the prophetic ministry are inseparable. The prophetic ministry cannot accomplish its full purpose without the Holy Spirit. Likewise, the Holy Spirit cannot fully reveal Christ apart from prophetic men and women who are yielded to Him for this purpose.

The Holy Spirit is vital to every believer, and to every ministry gift. But the Holy Spirit is uniquely aligned with the prophetic ministry in particular. Perhaps a pastor or teacher could occasionally get away with a message that is technically correct and "good" even while operating completely in the realm of the flesh or the mind, intellect or emotions. It happens all the time. But without the inspiration of the Holy Spirit, anyone attempting to speak prophetically is a pretender (at best) and a deceiver (at worst). The reason is simple: spiritual truth is hidden from the heart, mind, eyes, and ears of mortal man. Prophets can only see, hear, know, perceive, and discern whatever the Holy Spirit decides to reveal. Additionally, prophets can only declare what they have seen and heard by the power of the Holy Spirit. Thus, the Holy Spirit is the very life breath of the prophetic voice.

The primary purpose of the Holy Spirit is *not* to fill you with power. His purpose is to reveal Christ. When Christ is revealed, don't worry – the power will follow.

Similarly, the Holy Spirit was *not* sent just to give you spiritual gifts. His purpose is to reveal Christ as *the* Gift, the Source of every spiritual blessing, in Whom are hidden all the treasures of wisdom and knowledge. When Christ is revealed, believe me – the spiritual gifts will operate without any effort.

Likewise, the Holy Spirit was *not* sent only to bring you an occasional little word, dream, vision, or prophetic utterance. His purpose is to reveal Christ. When Christ is revealed, the word, dream, vision, and prophetic utterance will come bubbling forth – you won't be able to stop it.

Given the vital relationship that exists between the Holy Spirit and the prophetic ministry, it isn't enough for the prophet to be "filled" or even "led" by the Spirit; the prophet must be completely *governed* by the Holy Spirit. There is a lot packed into that word *governed* that must be pulled out and examined. What does it mean to be *governed by the Holy Spirit?* It includes the following seven steps, and each come in their proper order:

1. *Born of the Spirit.* This is where it all begins for "unless one is born of water and the Spirit, he cannot enter the kingdom of God." (Jn. 3:5). The Holy Spirit convicts us of sin, reveals our need for a Savior, draws us to Christ, enables us to call upon the Lord, and seals us with salvation. Apart from Him, we are blind, deaf, and dumb to the things of God, for "the natural man does not receive the things of the Spirit of God, for they are foolishness to him; nor can he know them, because they are spiritually discerned" (1 Cor. 2:14).

2. *Filled with the Spirit.* The remarkable difference in the disciples before and after Acts Chapter 2 is faithfully recorded in Scripture. The fact of the matter is: you can follow Jesus for years without being filled with the Holy Spirit, just like His first disciples did. But they were always limping along, not fully understanding, not completely seeing, not really hearing what Jesus wanted to show them. It took the Holy Spirit *filling* them before they could really begin to "get it." This accounts for the spiritual dullness of most people still trapped in Churchianity: they're trying to follow Jesus without the infilling power of the Holy Spirit. Scripture has already shown us it doesn't work; that's like trying

to run a marathon with asthma. We must "be *filled* with the Spirit" (Eph. 5:18).

3. *Taught by the Spirit.* Man can only teach us so much. The Spirit of Truth is a Teacher, and He is sent to show, reveal, and teach us things beyond the comprehension of mortal men. Many things that Jesus wished to teach His disciples had to wait because they could not receive it without the Holy Spirit there to assist. "But the Helper, the Holy Spirit, whom the Father will send in My name, He will teach you all things, and bring to your remembrance all things that I said to you" (Jn. 14:26). The Holy Spirit's favorite method of teaching is to put us in difficult circumstances. Read the Book of Acts and you see the rapid growth and development of the Ekklesia. Even the apostles are learning and growing. How do we account for it? Their learning didn't take place in a private mountain retreat or monastery, it happened through the trials and tribulations and enemies and circumstances. The Holy Spirit uses angry mobs, lonely prisons, and desperate situations to teach us things we won't learn in a classroom.

4. *Adjusted to the Spirit.* The Holy Spirit is not interested in filling our minds with interesting Bible facts and doctrinal trivia. The purpose of being taught by the Spirit is to be *adjusted* to the Spirit – that is, to give up our own stubborn way and come around to doing things God's way. This adjustment is usually uncomfortable and often painful. But this is how spiritual growth and maturity occurs. If we are not willing to take what the Spirit has taught us and then submit ourselves to it, and be *adjusted* by it, then we will go the way of those who are "ever learning, but never coming to the knowledge of the Truth" (2 Tim. 3:7). The Holy Spirit withdraws and will show us nothing beyond the last point of disobedience. We are the most taught and preached-to generation in the history of the world but we are the least willing to be *adjusted* by truth when we hear it. If we will learn to quickly obey and apply what we are taught, then we will make rapid progress.

5. *Led by the Spirit.* When a person is willing to be *adjusted* by the Spirit then they can be *led* by the Spirit. How can the Spirit lead a person that resists Him and refuses to be adjusted? It isn't possible. Yet how easily and flippantly people pronounce, "This is

how *I* am led!" as if that should settle all argument. Words may deceive, but the fruit doesn't lie. If the Spirit were actually leading everyone who claimed to be led by the Spirit then the world would be a lovely, wonderful place. The truth is: carnal, fleshly Christians can't be led by the Spirit because they won't be *taught* by the Spirit or *adjusted* to the Spirit. Carnal people are led by their flesh, their emotions, and their feelings. You can fool others, you can even fool yourself, but God is not mocked. You cannot ignore the Spirit's teaching, refuse the adjustment that the teaching is intended to make in your life, and then claim you're being "led" by the same Spirit you just disrespected. Only those who are adjusted to the Spirit can truly recognize His voice and be led by Him.

6. *Inspired by the Spirit.* When a person arrives at this point they have learned to originate nothing, but to wait for the inspiration of the Holy Spirit. They are under the government of the Holy Spirit from that point forward. The Spirit governs their speech and their actions. They no longer rely on the flesh. They no longer relish the praise of man, nor fear the criticisms of man. They are stirred by the Spirit of God, and they offer no resistance

to His Spirit. They can be trusted with greater revelation and with the corresponding responsibility for handling it wisely, as a stewardship for the Ekklesia.

7. *Kept by the Spirit.* The Holy Spirit continually ministers life, light, love, grace, mercy, and peace to those who are wholly submitted to His Government. The inner man is strengthened and renewed day by day. Rivers of living water flow from within. The spiritual fruit bears evidence of a life submitted to Christ: love, joy, peace, patience, kindness, goodness, faithfulness, gentleness and self control are witnessed in ever-increasing quantities. The battles are great, but His grace is greater, and His power is perfected in weakness. They are kept by the Spirit – reserved for His use, set apart for holy purposes, sealed, anointed, and empowered.

If there is a shortage of genuine prophets in the Ekklesia now, it is largely because most people stumble and fall somewhere between Step Three and Step Four and proceed no further. If they try to press forward in the flesh (or get sucked into religious leadership) then they become false prophets somewhere around Steps Five and Six, following all sorts of false leadings and being inspired either by their own imagination or by a demonic spirit. Step Seven is completely unknown to them.

The critical junction is the willingness to *apply* what the Holy Spirit teaches, and a readiness to be *adjusted* to His Word and His Way. When the Spirit whispers, we must be quick to say, "Yes, Lord; Your servant is listening. What would You have me to do?" Then we must be quick to obey. There is no limit to what God can do in and through a person who is unreservedly committed to His Government.

Prophetic Requirement #2 – Receives Revelation, Discernment, Insight, and Wisdom Concerning the Heart, Mind, Will and Purposes of God Concerning Christ

We have previously stated that the prophet *receives* from the Holy Spirit and *declares* it to others. *Revelation* is received; once the revelation is declared to others, we refer to it as *testimony*. The essence of the prophetic word is the *Testimony* of Jesus – the declaration of what has been revealed as true concerning Christ. Peter and John alluded to this when they said, "We cannot but speak the things which we have seen and heard" (Acts 4:20). They have seen and heard something – that is *revelation*. Now they cannot help but speak it – that is *testimony*. So the prophetic ministry requires men and women who can handle both the receiving and the giving effectively.

Let us first deal with revelation. Receiving revelation is something of an art. To intentionally seek revelation is one thing that sets the prophet apart from the ordinary person who passively waits to receive. The prophet does not wait for revelation, but pursues it. The prophetic person asks, seeks, knocks and pays the price until revelation is obtained. There are many forms in which the revelation comes, and the prophetic person does not limit themselves to one or two ways, but hears and sees through many different means. Following is a partial list of forms in which revelation is communicated to the prophet, beginning with the most basic, and working up to the most advanced.

1. *Written Scripture.* Scripture is the objective criterion against which all subjective revelation is measured, weighed, tested, and interpreted. That is to say, the Holy Spirit will not reveal something to a prophet that contradicts what has already been revealed in Scripture. "Forever, O Lord, Your Word is settled in heaven" (Ps. 119:89). The prophetic word is rooted in the written Word, and that Word is settled forever. We must submit ourselves to His Word, and not try to make the Word submit to us or to our revelation. Take for an example the prophet Daniel. Daniel began to fast and pray after he "*learned from reading the word of the Lord, as revealed to Jeremiah the prophet*, that

Jerusalem must lie desolate for seventy years" (Dan. 9:2). To reward Daniel's willingness to search for answers and to pray, God gave Daniel a vision that supported the written revelation of Jeremiah. Now both Jeremiah and Daniel's prophecies are part of Scripture. Study that example and you will save yourself from a lot of unnecessary confusion and misunderstanding. The prophet must avoid the realm of speculation and learn not to go beyond what is written (1 Cor. 4:6). This is good advice, not just for prophets, but for all of God's people. We must master the written revelation, as this will be the basis upon which we will approve or reject any subsequent revelation.

2. *Inward Witness.* How does God give us specific guidance about matters not spoken of in Scripture? He uses the *inward witness* (or "gentle nudging") of the Holy Spirit. How does one know to go here, or look there, or study this, or dig deeper into that, or pray about this particular matter? Where do these sparks of inspiration and insight come from? They come from the Holy Spirit, as He seeks to lead us into all truth. Sometimes these leadings are barely noticeable, almost as if you were thinking to yourself. At other times, these leadings

are genuine "light bulb" moments when you slap yourself on the forehead and exclaim, "Of course! Why didn't I see that before?" This may appear to be in the realm of the mind, and the mind is certainly involved, but it actually originates in the realm of the spirit, where the Holy Spirit moves and "the eyes of your understanding are enlightened" (Eph. 1:18). The key is to take none of this for granted. Treasure all these little insights and store them away in your heart.

3. *Word of Wisdom/Word of Knowledge.* Any of God's people may operate in spiritual gifts as the Spirit wills, but the prophet seems to flow in these spiritual gifts more often than most. We must not limit our understanding of the spiritual gifts to what we have seen allegedly demonstrated on television, or in church services and revival meetings. Words of wisdom and knowledge do not have to be uttered to be valid, and they do not always have to be directed towards other people. They are simply Spirit-inspired fragments of insight into things past, present, or future: thus, it is a "word" of wisdom, or a "word" of knowledge, but it is not total wisdom or full knowledge. These fragments are typically used as calls to prayer, or perhaps specific

answers to prayer, or specific insights. The key word is *specific*. When Jesus told the Samaritan woman that, "You have well said, 'I have no husband.' For you have had five husbands, and the man with whom you are living now is not your husband" (Jn. 4:17,18), she immediately perceived Him as a prophet. The word was specific and correct. It both exposed her and opened up the opportunity to minister to her.

4. *Visions and Dreams.* In the Old Testament, visions and dreams were more common because prophets did not enjoy the indwelling presence of the Holy Spirit as we do. To communicate, God often had to take direct measures to get His point across, whereas today (I believe) God prefers to use Scripture and the Inward Witness as the primary means of revelation. That is not to say that visions and dreams are not valid for us today. Paul dreamed that a man from Macedonia was calling to him for help, and he correctly concluded that God was sending him there to preach (Acts 16:9,10). God does use the occasional dream or vision to communicate revelation; however, not all dreams and visions are of divine origin. We must be sensible enough to test all things.

5. *Other People.* We can learn to recognize and hear God's voice speaking to us through other people. Of course this includes older brothers and sisters and those who are pastors, teachers, and the like. But God can speak through anyone – young or old, believer or unbeliever. For example, God often speaks to me through other people, even when they do not realize He is using them to speak to me. And even though I may be "older" in the Lord and a teacher, I have things to learn from those who are younger. Even our critics and "enemies" (according to the flesh) can be used by God to teach and reveal truth to us. So we must not limit ourselves to thinking that God must always speak directly to us and would never speak *through* someone else. This attitude would almost certainly guarantee that God will use someone else to help you get over this self-centered view. On the other hand, if we are always looking to other people for guidance then it represents a flaw in our walk that must be corrected.

6. *Prophecy.* We would not want to overlook the fact that personal words of prophecy, encouragement, and counsel are possible means of revelation and guidance. We must test these words, ensure they do not violate

Scripture, and receive them to the extent that they confirm what the Lord has already been showing us. If these words from others create confusion or intimidation then we can safely ignore them. God has other ways and means of getting our attention if He really needs to.

7. *"The Hard Way"*. This is the most challenging way to receive revelation – and by far, the most effective. Paul had a deep revelation of Christ. He also endured deep suffering. In fact, the abundance of his revelation required a corresponding "messenger of satan" to keep him humble (2 Cor. 12:7). Whatever this means, we can rest assured of one thing: Deep revelation is accompanied by deep suffering. Those who aspire to apostolic and prophetic revelation must be willing to endure apostolic and prophetic persecution. Does the revelation trigger the suffering, or does the suffering trigger the revelation? The answer is: both. If our suffering is light then our revelation will be shallow, but deep experiences lead to deep revelation, and deep revelation leads to deep experiences. The messenger is as much a part of the message as the message itself. It is a 100% certainty that the prophetic man

or woman will experience deep testing and trials as part of their training.

Prophetic Requirement #3 – Declares this Revelation to Others by the Inspiration of the Holy Spirit

Now we turn to the final requirement: what has been revealed must eventually be *declared* to others. For the ordinary person, revelation received may be stored up or used. But the prophet receives all revelation as a stewardship to the Ekklesia; meaning, the revelation is not given for the private benefit of the prophet, but is intended for the ultimate well-being and spiritual maturity of the entire Body of Christ. For this revelation to benefit anyone else, it must be communicated to others.

This can be likened to speaking in tongues. In First Corinthians 14, Paul explains that the one who speaks in an unknown tongue edifies themselves, while the one who interprets what is said edifies the Ekklesia. The unknown tongue is like personal revelation: it is hidden, secret, and unknown to others; therefore, while the one with the revelation is edified, it benefits no one else. But if someone interprets the unknown tongue, that which was previously hidden can now be known by others, and all are edified. This is what the prophetic person does when taking revelation and interpreting it for others, transforming it into a *testimony* that edifies all.

As with receiving revelation, there are numerous ways to make the revelation known. A few are listed below. As before, we begin with the most basic methods and progress to the more advanced.

1. *Declaring the Goodness of God.* This is what first comes to mind when you think of a person giving their "testimony" or "witnessing." This can be done in a way that lifts up Self, or in a way that lifts up Christ. When it lifts up Christ, it takes on a prophetic quality. After hearing the person share, you have the sense that you have witnessed Christ in the person. When the new believers prophesied and spoke in tongues in Acts 2, it says the people heard them proclaiming the mighty works of God. This speaking is inspired by the Holy Spirit and edifies others. It qualifies as prophetic because it reveals Christ.

2. *Prayer.* Most prayer is concerned with asking for needs to be met. This kind of prayer has its place, but there is a higher place of prayer. The prophetic form of prayer is more concerned with the ultimate purpose and intention of God being fulfilled: "Your Kingdom come, and Your Will be done; on earth, as it is in heaven" (Mt. 6:10). It is standing in the gap and

offering intercessory prayer for the Ekklesia and for the world. Only those with revelation can consistently rise up and pray in this manner. In this case, the revelation is declared in the prayers that are prayed. Daniel is a good example of what it means to pray prophetically.

3. *Singing / Worship.* The Book of Psalms is filled with prophetic revelations of Christ and the Kingdom of God. David was not only a musician, psalmist, and poet, he was also a prophet who declared the purposes of God concerning Christ (Acts 2:29,30). Many prophetic people express revelation through music, poems, and art. So long as it is inspired by the Holy Spirit and reveals Christ, it is prophetic. Keith Green is a good example of a man I consider to be a singing prophet of the order of David. Though he is no longer with us in the flesh, his songs remain as a musical Testimony of Jesus.

4. *Prophesying.* One of the most common means of declaring revelation is through the spoken word. John the Baptist was described as "a voice in the wilderness, crying 'Prepare the way of the Lord'" (Mk. 1:3). In the age before mass communication and sophisticated writing conventions, verbal communication was the preferred

method. But not all prophesying can be done verbally; sometimes the prophet must commit the prophetic word to...

5. *Writing*. When Jeremiah the prophet was banned from entering the Temple, he dictated his prophetic words to Baruch the scribe. Baruch copied everything into a scroll, went to the Temple on behalf of Jeremiah, and began reading the prophecies out loud to the people. The written word was as convicting as the spoken word; the people were fearful, and the king cut up the scroll and burned it. The Lord told Jeremiah to dictate it to Baruch again, and a second version of the same scroll was written. But this second version had an additional word of judgment especially for the king (see Jeremiah 36)! So writing is a valuable means of prophetic declaration. When Paul could no longer travel (being a prisoner of Rome) he began to write the letters that form most of our New Testament. Many years ago, when the church I was involved with was afraid to let me preach, I found that writing was the only way to relieve the burden of the Lord. The written word can travel to places that the spoken word cannot go.

6. *Teaching.* If prophesying is *proclaiming*, then teaching is *explaining*. Not all teachers are prophets, and not all prophets are teachers. But teaching is a powerful means through which prophetic truths can be revealed, declared and *explained* to others. The assumption that all prophetic revelation is somehow beyond explanation isn't true. "These things we also speak, not in words which man's wisdom teaches but which the Holy Spirit teaches, comparing spiritual things with spiritual" (1 Cor. 2:13). Both the mind and the spirit are exercised in prophetic teaching, and this is critically important. God's people need to *discern*, yes; but they also need to *think* and *know* in order to reach spiritual adulthood. Skilled prophetic teaching is just another way to help the Ekklesia grow in wisdom so that they can comprehend the heart, mind, will and purpose of God for our age.

7. *Parable & Proverb.* Jesus was a master of parables and proverbs. Those who were serious would seek Him out for the explanation, and He would take them deeper. Those who were not serious would pursue it no further. There is a danger in telling everyone everything we think we know. It is much better to give hints and clues that allow people to come to their

own conclusions. For example, when David sinned with Bathsheba, the prophet Nathan went to David and told him a parable about a rich man who stole a poor man's lamb. David angrily pronounced judgment on the rich man in the story; then Nathan said, "You are that man!" (2 Sam. 12:7). Had Nathan confronted David directly, David might have become defensive and made excuses. But with this indirect approach, David condemned himself, and his eyes were opened. Parables and proverbs are used to stir up the listener to think, to pray, to exercise their heart, or to seek deeper truth. Why not speak plainly? Because the timing may be wrong, or the person may be unprepared for the full weight of the truth. Perhaps you are only supposed to provide one piece of the puzzle, but they have to put it together. Sometimes God simply wishes to keep some things sealed for the time being (Rev. 10:4). The prophet is careful not to reveal too much, too soon.

8. *Meaningful Acts.* There is a reason *why* Jesus cursed the fig tree. It was not merely a display of His power: it was an act that had prophetic significance and meaning. In this case, it was far more effective to *show* than to *tell.* This prophetic act reinforced the prophetic word that followed and made

it all the more memorable and full of impact.

9. *Signs.* "Truly Jesus did many other signs in the presence of His disciples, which are not written in this book" (Jn. 20:30). Signs are unusual, remarkable demonstrations of power that authenticate God's messengers. It is interesting that Jesus only performed signs *in the presence of His disciples*; when outsiders pressed Him for a sign, He refused to accommodate them (Mk. 8:12). This indicates that prophetic signs are divine confirmations *for those who already believe*; they are not intended to persuade skeptics. Indeed, Jesus warns that false prophets will come in His name and show "signs and wonders" in an effort to *prove* their authenticity, thus giving themselves away as false (Mt. 24:24).

10. *Miracles.* Moses and Elijah come to mind immediately as prophets who backed up their prophetic messages with miracles. While this is certainly in the realm of possibility for prophets today, it is not a requirement that prophets be miracle-workers. John the Baptist is described by Jesus as "the greatest prophet" (Lk. 7:28), and yet "John did no miracles" (Jn. 10:41)! John was the greatest prophet because he

had the clearest revelation of Christ and he declared Him so plainly and consistently. While all who preceded him saw in part and prophesied in part, John saw clearly – summing up the entire plan and purpose of God in seven simple words of prophetic testimony: "He must increase, but I must decrease" (Jn. 3:30).

* * * *

To summarize: the prophet is uniquely called to discern and declare, by the inspiration of the Holy Spirit, the purposes of God concerning Christ. The prophetic ministry is one of the five-fold ministry gifts, given by God for the edification of the Ekklesia. The prophet must therefore fulfill the general requirements of the five-fold ministry as well as the specific requirements unique to his or her prophetic function. The prophet must be wholly governed by the Holy Spirit, and the prophet receives revelation and declares testimony by the inspiration of the same Spirit. All is done for the benefit of the Ekklesia.

God takes great care to mold and shape His messengers into trustworthy vessels. May the Lord give us the discernment to *recognize* them – and the humility to *receive* from them.

Chapter Three

A Hidden Ministry

"And the child Samuel ministered to the Lord before Eli. The word of the Lord was rare in those days, and there was no revelation" (1 Sam. 3:1).

W hat does it mean to be the Lord's minister and prophet? What is ministry? According to the popular definition of ministry I have actually been "in the ministry" for many years. I have always been in a state of either preparing for the ministry or performing ministry as I understood it. Of course, that means I have either been pastoring a church, teaching a class, or operating some kind of evangelistic or missionary outreach. This is what comes to mind when most people think of the word "ministry." It is the working definition I operated from for the majority of my life.

Through a series of painful experiences the Lord brought me to a deeper understanding of what ministry to Him is. In this chapter I would like to explain this deeper ministry. I have referred to it a number of times in other writings and in my spoken messages, but by the grace of the Lord I would like to take some time here and expound a bit on this perspective of ministry.

This ministry actually existed before anything else came into being, so it is not new at all, but it is certainly rare, so it may be new to us, though it is old. Simply defined, this is ministry that is directed *to the Lord.* Whereas typical ministry is directed *to* man and *for* man, the ministry of which I am speaking is directed *to* the Lord and *for* the Lord. There is a place for ministry to the saints, yet there are many instances and examples of ministry to the saints, and very few instances of ministry *to the Lord alone.* I understand that most people minister to men "for the Lord's sake" and see it as one and the same; nevertheless, I am speaking of a kind of ministry that is *wholly* for the Lord, and not for man at all. Ministry to men is commonplace, but ministry to the Lord is on the verge of extinction.

Even as I write these words I realize that not everyone will understand or accept what has to be said. I am not trying to convince anyone to change anything. But I believe the Lord has always reserved for Himself people who will minister *to Him*, especially at this time when the Lord's need is so urgent. With a little light thrown on the subject you may at last hear the confirmation you need to be released into this fullness. So those who are meant to hear this will hear it, and you know who you are. The rest of you may take it as another "interesting study" and go along as before. But it is my prayer that as we consider the Scriptures together, the Lord will use this to confirm what He has been saying to many of you already. He is indeed drawing many saints into this ministry. So let us explore it together with open hearts and open minds to see what the Lord is saying to us.

The Basis of God's Need: A Love Relationship

> "This is a great mystery, but I speak concerning Christ and the Church" (Eph. 5:32).

Before we go any further we need to stop and explain what is meant by "The Lord's Need." Some hear it for the first time and think we are suggesting that the Lord has some kind of a lack that makes Him incomplete, and thus, not all-powerful. That is not what we are saying at all.

We have to think about the Lord's Need, not in terms of His ability or omnipotence, but in terms of His heart's desire. I do not "need" my wife. I can dress myself, feed myself, and take care of myself just fine. I can exist apart from her. But in another sense I do need my wife, and I do not want to exist apart from her. From a relationship standpoint, from a love perspective, I need her. In the same way, God is God with us or without us. But from the point of view of a love relationship, God has a Purpose, a Desire, and yes, a Need. There is something that will satisfy His heart that only we can provide, and that something is beyond description, except to say it has to do with love. It has to do with our response to His overtures towards us. Proverbs tells us that love is too wonderful to understand or explain (Prov. 30:18,19). In fact, the only reason why God continued beyond the creation of angels and animals, towards something closer to His own image, was to have someone whom He could love (and be loved) on the same level as Himself, and that is only possible when He is able to fill that person completely. In other words, they must be made in His image, and they must be changed into His likeness.

It is all about relationship! Look at how Eve came forth from Adam. First, there was a need. "It is not good for Adam to be alone." Then, all the animals were brought to Adam, but a suitable help-meet was not found among them. Then, Eve was created out of Adam, and at last the need was met, for "she is bone of my bone, and flesh of my flesh" (cf. Gen. 2). Paul says this explains the mystery of Christ and the Church (Eph. 5:30-32). How so? It is a pattern of the heavenly relationship. First, if we may boldly say, the Lord decided it was not good for Him to be alone anymore! We will have to explain that further as we go along. In any event, the angels and animals were created, but a suitable help-meet was not found among them. If they were suitable then He would have stopped there, but they did not and could not fully meet His Need or satisfy His Desire. Instead, God took something of Himself and created Man in His own image – someone who would be a little below the angels and a little above the animals. Now, we are "members of His Body, of His flesh, and of His bones" (Eph. 5:30).

Did not Christ, the pre-existent Son, satisfy God's heart? Indeed. But if we look at the language of Genesis, we see, "Let *us* make man in *our* own image" (Gen. 1:26a). God the Father, God the Son, and God the Holy Spirit together desired for companionship and communion with someone other than themselves. Hence, it was agreed to proceed with the creation of a being that would have the capacity for giving and receiving love in a way that is quite beyond the reach of animals or angels. And so we have the creation of Man. If we look back over the history of mankind we see the tremendous energy and exertion put forth by the Godhead to create Man, then redeem him after he sinned, in order to restore this rocky relationship. What a tremendous cost was involved! What an awesome price was to be paid! What plausible explanation is there to justify all the time, effort, trouble, and longsuffering God has had to endure in His dealings with Man? How are we to understand the willingness of Christ to die for us?

The only thing that makes sense is totally illogical, yet understandable. Only someone *in love* would put themselves through such trouble. So in God's case it is *love*, deeper than we can fathom, that motivates Him. Therefore, to meet the Lord's Need is to satisfy His heart's desire for communion and fellowship on a level that is beyond our own abilities. How then can we do it? Such communion can only truly occur when Christ has the preeminence in us, for He is the only One Who, *as a Man*, has ever completely met the Lord's Need and satisfied His heart. Others have come close.

> "You cannot truly love until you know God, for God is love" (1 Jn. 4:8).

Imagine, if you can, what it must be like to have so much to give, so much to share, so much love to pour out, but no one around who can receive it, appreciate it, benefit from it, or even know that such love exists. God *is* love. Can we imagine what it must be like to *be* love, but have no one to love? An omnipotent, omniscient, omnipresent, eternal God Who is Love is in some unimaginable sense incomplete without someone who can represent the object of His love, adoration, tender mercies, and personal care. We talk about a God-shaped vacuum in every man's heart that only God can fill. Is it too much to imagine that perhaps there is a man-shaped vacuum in God's heart that only man can fill? If this is so, then union with God is as much about meeting *God's* need as it is about meeting *man's* need.

If this seems far-fetched, consider God's initial reaction to mankind as a whole when it became clear that sin had consumed them all. Scripture says that when God saw that every imagination and thought of man was only towards evil continually, He was grieved in His heart (Gen. 6:6). The Hebrew word "grieved" here is a rich, full word that carries with it many emotions, including worry, anger, grief, and (here is what I want us to see) *hurt*. God was brokenhearted! Why this flood of emotion? Of course, there is the obvious fact that men have fallen into sin and are killing one another. "God hates sin!" the preachers scream. Everyone knows that God hates sin – but *why* does He hate sin?

Here is a picture of what Sin really is. The Lord comes down to commune with the man in the cool of the day, as usual. But this time the man is nowhere to be found. So the Lord begins to call out, "Where are you?" The man, shaking and trembling in the bushes, is too afraid to come out and commune with God as before (cf. Gen. 3). The man has lost something priceless – but can you not see that the Lord has lost just as much? Friends, *that* is what makes sin such a hateful thing to God. It makes people hide from God so that God is left by Himself, calling out to people who are too afraid to respond. There are billions of people on the earth today, and most of them are hiding in the bushes while God calls out to them. Is this not a pitiful situation? Then what truly grieves God the most? That the *one being* in all of creation with whom He may have a close relationship does not have Him in their thoughts at all; indeed, they are running in the opposite direction, quite oblivious to the Lord, quite apathetic to His desire towards them, quite complacent to seeking Him at all, quite afraid to even respond if they knew how.

If there is anything worse than having no one to love, it would have to be loving someone and seeing that love ignored altogether. This brings us to a very important characteristic of love: whenever we love someone, we essentially give them the power to hurt us. If you ask a parent what is their greatest source of pleasure and pain they will say it is their kids. If we dare to love someone, or care for them, or watch over them, or if we dare take responsibility for bringing life into the world, then we are making ourselves vulnerable to being hurt by the very thing we love. This explains why some people swear never to love again once they have been hurt by a relationship. If love is that painful, why love at all? Because love is so great that it is better to love with the chance of being hurt than to not love at all. It underscores just how risky love can be.

> "We love Him, because He first loved us" (1 Jn. 4:19).

The problems of free moral agency and sin came into being precisely because of this love. In order for man to love God he must have the freedom to choose this relationship. If it is forced upon him in an involuntary way then it is not true love. In other words, I cannot "make" my wife love me. Any attempt on my part to force her to love me will result in something that is not love. When we fall in love with someone we cannot be absolutely sure that they will fall in love with us. So man must be free to love God or to not love God – again, one of the risks that love takes. With this freedom there is the possibility that man will choose to walk his own path away from God and fall into sin. As we all know, this is exactly what happened.

So God took a huge risk in wanting us as the object of His affection, and from the very beginning we have failed Him. Of course, He already knew that we would fail, which is why He made provision for our sin before we ever sinned. But why pay such a high price? Why does He continue to love us? Why not just give up? Because unlike our best attempts at love, He is Perfect Love, and this Love eventually wins. This Love never fails. He cannot stop trying. If we would read the Bible, especially the prophetic Scriptures, and treat it as a love letter from a husband to an unfaithful wife, or a frustrated parent to a wayward child, we would begin to understand the Lord's heart. For six thousand years of human history the Lord has spoken, pleaded, argued, grieved, wooed, reprimanded, remonstrated, and reasoned with man in order to have what He has wanted all along – a relationship, a companionship, a camaraderie, a communion with those made in His image.

With all of this background, let us digress a bit now and observe how the gospel is presented to people today. This "gospel" only provides people with half of the story: the half that benefits them. How much effort is made to show people what the Lord has lost, and what the Lord stands to gain, by sinners coming to Christ, and by Christians growing up into the full-knowledge (*epignosis*) of Him? Very little attention is given to ministering to the Lord or meeting the Lord's Need (most have never heard about the Lord's Need, and those who have are still questioning it; we have a long way to go). Instead, the Gospel as it is presented today is primarily concerned with man and how to meet his needs – how to escape hell, go to heaven, be healed, be blessed, be victorious, be prosperous, be fulfilled, be happy, be anointed, etc. etc. ad infinitum. This has, of course, created a paradigm in which we see God as being there to meet our needs, minister to us, guide us through the difficulties of life, and prepare a place for us to go when we die. It is no wonder that few have ears to hear when we discuss ministering to the Lord. It represents something totally foreign to the Christian experience as they have known it and seen it up until now.

As "advanced" as our Western culture seems to be, this kind of one-way, egocentric, "what can I get out of it" relationship is not too unlike the relationship that pagans and heathens have with their animistic gods and idols. They keep their gods appeased, not because they love them, but because they have some self-serving need they want met, whether it is health, prosperity, rain, or protection from their enemies. How is this different than the Gospel according to Churchianity? We pay tithes, apply the Blood, dispatch the angels, pray the Prayer of Jabez, and get the "Anointing" so that things will go well with us, too. It falls way, way short of the mark.

The model we give to people of "a personal relationship with Christ" is so dysfunctional and self-centered it would not keep a human marriage together for a week; so why do we keep relating to Him this way? "We *love* Him," the Scriptures declare, "*because* He first loved us." Real communion, real worship, real fellowship, real relationship with God is based upon meeting His Need, i.e., providing Him with heart-satisfaction by responding in kind to His overtures of love towards us. It says in effect, "How can I help but love Him, now that I see how much He loves me? How can I ignore Him any longer?" This is followed by, "You love me so much, You have done so much for me, that I am content with You, and I desire nothing else but You. You have satisfied my heart; now how can I satisfy Your Heart? How can I minister to You? What is Your Desire? Not my will, but Your Will. I love you, Lord!" Thus, we minister to Him, and after an eternity of waiting the Lord has finally broken through and gained the relationship He has for so long sought you out for.

How refreshing, how delightful, how wonderful this kind of relationship is! Is there anyone who has ever lived like this? YES! Let us look at some of them right now.

Samuel

> "And the child Samuel ministered to the Lord before Eli. The word of the Lord was rare in those days, and there was no revelation" (1 Sam. 3:1).

The third chapter of First Samuel is so rich. If we want to talk about prophetic integrity, prophetic calling, and prophetic formation then there is no better place to go. In the beginning of the chapter we see that a true word from the Lord was rare in those days. We see Samuel ministering to the Lord as a child, and the Lord calling out to Samuel. After some initial confusion Samuel received the word of the Lord. There is the reluctance to give it, and finally the obedience of telling Eli "every whit" of what the Lord had shown him. By the end of the chapter the prophetic calling of Samuel is established, his words never fall to the ground, and the Lord reveals Himself to Samuel completely.

Can you see the progression here? We begin with no revelation, and we end with the Lord revealing Himself. We begin with the Lord closed off from man, and end with the Lord opening Himself up to a man, and by extension, to the rest of the nation through this man. We begin with a child, and end with a prophet. Let us look at the last verse of chapter three and quote it together with the first verse of chapter four: "And the Lord appeared again in Shiloh: for the Lord revealed Himself to Samuel in Shiloh by the word of the Lord. And the word of Samuel came to all Israel..." (1 Sam. 3:21-4:1a).

Notice the word of the Lord came to Samuel, then the word of Samuel came to Israel. I wonder if we can grasp the significance of this! The Lord has committed Himself to a man, and the man has committed himself to the Lord. Thus, the word of the Lord to Samuel becomes the word of Samuel to Israel. The Lord did not speak to Israel directly, but He spoke to Samuel, who then spoke in the name of the Lord to Israel. My point is this: what is the foundation upon which this close relationship is built? How did it get its start? "The child Samuel ministered to the Lord." Who is the friend of God? Who knows God? Who hears from God? Who speaks for God? The one who ministers to Him, who seeks His face, who is aligned with His desire, who seeks His satisfaction, who meets His need.

In every respect the times in which we live are comparable to 1 Samuel 3. A genuine word from God is rare, and there is no open vision. In other words, most of the people who see something do not have revelation to really know what they are seeing – hence it remains closed, or worse, it is misinterpreted and becomes a delusion. There is an abundance of words, dreams, visions, and prophecies today, but I repeat: a *genuine* word from God is rare, and there is little *revelation.* Do you understand my meaning? And the priesthood as represented by Eli is old, fat, and blind: operating as always, still standing in the place of the priest, but already under judgment. What is the problem? No one ministers to the Lord. Everyone is for themselves. Except for one child who ministers to the Lord – and *that* is the one to whom the Lord revealed Himself. There is no revelation apart from relationship. I learned this the hard way.

David

> "The Lord has sought for Himself a man after His own heart" (1 Sam. 13:14ff).

> "And the Lord said to Samuel, 'Why do you keep mourning over Saul? I have rejected him from ruling Israel! Now get up, take your oil, and go. I am sending you to Jesse in Bethlehem, for I have found Me a king among his sons... for the Lord sees not as man sees, for man looks on the outward appearance, but I look upon the heart'" (1 Sam. 16:1,7b).

Samuel is significant because the Lord used him to locate and call forth another one who, better than anyone else, represents what it means to minister to the Lord. This man, David, was so determined to minister to the Lord that he invented musical instruments to worship God with. He wrote songs to the Lord on these instruments and was a zealous worshipper, and we still have a record of his writings in the Book of Psalms, revered by the Christian and Jew alike.

What I want us to see here is that the Lord was seeking out David just as much as David was seeking out the Lord. "The Lord has sought for Himself..." The Lord's Need is expressed very succinctly in this phrase. We should not imagine a passive God who sits benignly in the heavens, waiting to see if anyone is going to worship Him or not. This is a proactive God, Who seeks Spirit-and-Truth worshippers, Who seeks people after His own heart, Who draws people to Himself, Who reveals Himself insofar as we will allow Him, Who is ready to speak insofar as we will listen. What a mighty God! What an awesome thing this is: "I have sought for Myself a man, someone who will want Me for Who I am, someone who seeks what I seek, who will obey Me fully, who will love Me unreservedly, who will follow Me wholeheartedly, so that I can give Myself completely to him in return."

And what could be better than this? "I have found Me a king." The Lord has sought for Himself a man, and has found for Himself a king. The Lord found what He was looking for, and as we follow David's path we find that David, too, had found a King. Look at the sensitivity of David in 2 Samuel 7. He wanted to build a house for God, and God said that He would instead build a house for David. As David pondered this we learn from the Psalms that the House is the Church, and the Son Who will reign forever is not Solomon, but

Christ. Peter called David a prophet who saw the resurrection of Christ (Acts 2:29,30). In fact, David clearly saw the incarnation (Ps. 8), the crucifixion (Ps. 22), the death (Ps. 88), the ascension (Ps. 68), the resurrection (Ps. 16), and the reign of Christ (Ps. 2). How deep was his revelation! How vast was his vision! The one who seeks the heart of God will see as God sees. Write it down and underline it: *no relationship, no revelation.*

Anna

> "And there was one Anna, a prophetess... a widow eighty-four years old, who never left the Temple, but served God with fastings and prayers night and day" (Lk. 2:36,37).

While we have a full account of King David's life, we know very little about Anna. She was the daughter of Phanuel, of the tribe of Asher, and lived with her husband only seven years before she became a widow. Now she was eighty-four years old. Perhaps the experience of losing her husband after such a brief time together helped forge the character of this prophetess. We have no way of knowing.

We have no record of any prophetic words or visions or dreams from Anna. How can you have a prophetess who does not prophesy? Quite simply, because the prophetic ministry is something more vast than being able to give out a few "words" from God. The only thing we know about Anna's ministry is that it was primarily devoted to ministering to the Lord with unceasing fasting and prayer. We might consider this monastic, yet the Bible considers this prophetic.

We are not suggesting that to minister to the Lord means to neglect people altogether. There is no need to force such an unnecessary dichotomy. But we maintain that there can be no real Spirit-and-Truth ministry to people until and unless we have first ministered to the Lord. For one thing, we cannot be motivated by man's need, but by God's Need, because often the two are in conflict. And, we cannot speak Life except by revelation, and this we can only receive from God.

Unless we have invested a great deal of time in our secret ministry to the Lord then the shallowness of our public ministry will be very evident. Today it is abundantly clear that not enough time is spent ministering to the Lord, and way too much time is spent ministering to people; hence, most of what is done in the name of ministry is performed in a fleshly, human way which never bears any lasting fruit.

There in the Temple, Anna ministered to the Lord. She never wrote a book, never had a website, never conducted a meeting that we can tell. All in all it seems to be a very passive existence, the sort of "waste" that makes us want to criticize her for not being more useful. Anna the prophetess should be "doing" something.

But how many of us consider prayer and fasting to be serving God? We cannot repeat often enough that for too many people, prayer and fasting is a way to serve *themselves*, or to get God involved in *their* cause.

We have a need, so we pray, and if the need is critical and we become desperate, then we will fast. This may be appropriate in some situations, but it is not serving the *Lord*. It may be done to bring about *our* will, but it is not necessarily motivated by a desire to minister to the Lord, to see His heart satisfied, and to see His Need met.

Now it is no coincidence that, in verse 38, Anna came "in that instant" and met Simeon, Joseph, Mary, and the baby Jesus in the Temple, and recognized Him to be the Christ. In response, she "gave thanks to the Lord and spoke of Him to all that looked for redemption in Jerusalem." Jesus is only a few days old here. There are no angelic choirs singing "Hosanna", no shepherds bowing down to worship, no star blazing overhead. All the outward signs have disappeared, and this Baby seems to be no different in outward appearance than the dozens of other Jewish babies being dedicated in the Temple that day.

But Anna knew the difference because she devoted her life to ministering to the Lord. What seems like a waste turned out to be the very thing that put her in the right place at the right time, while the more "useful" busybodies missed the entire event.

Again, we find that prophetic things, revelatory things, are inescapably linked to ministering to the Lord. No relationship, no revelation.

The Twelve Disciples

> "And Jesus ordained twelve, that they should be with Him, and that He might send them forth to preach" (Mk. 3:14).

I taught from this passage of Scripture at a minister's retreat once in order to demonstrate to them that whatever they thought their ministry was, be it as an apostle, prophet, evangelist, pastor or teacher, their first calling was not to be with people at all, but to be with Jesus. How simple this is. Twelve men are ordained, or set apart, or selected. For what? To preach? Eventually, but not immediately. To save sinners? Eventually, but not immediately. To work miracles? Eventually, but not immediately.

The immediate Need was for those who would just *be with the Lord.* They were set apart to be with Him; their being sent forth (*apostello*) was of secondary concern. It would follow, but it was not the most important thing. The most important thing was that they *be with the Lord.* Where has "the ministry" failed? In putting people before the Lord, in making the work of the Lord more important than the Lord of the work, in being so busy with preaching and visitation and building programs and church administration and a thousand and one things that there is no time to *be with the Lord.*

I learned many years ago that it does not matter how busy I am for God, or how many things I am doing in the Name of Jesus, or how much I am able to bless other people, if I am not "with Jesus" on a continual basis. How easy it is to be absorbed, obsessed, and consumed with our little ministry, our little work, our little church, and forget that the whole reason we are called in the first place is to minister to the Lord, to be with Him, to love Him. Are we in love with the Lord, or are we in love with the Lord's work? Are we motivated by the Lord's Need, or by man's need? If the Lord told us to come aside for a year, leave our ministry alone, and just be with Him, would it bring us great joy or would we argue that we are engaged in such an important work that we cannot stop?

Is it possible that long ago we became so entrenched in the work of the Lord that He is no longer involved in what we are doing? Could it be that we are now proceeding in our own strength, in our own name, according to flesh and blood? The fruit of our labor (or the lack thereof) tells the whole story. If spiritual fruit is defined by how many people are saved, how many churches are planted, how many sermons are preached, then we can bring forth that kind of fruit and never involve the Lord at all. But if spiritual fruit is love, joy, peace, patience, gentleness, goodness, faith, meekness, and self-control, then we must be with Jesus in order to bring forth this fruit, and no amount of *working* for God can make up for a lack of simply *being* with Him.

Ministry to the Lord in Antioch

> "There were in the ekklesia at Antioch certain prophets and teachers... and as they ministered to the Lord, and fasted, the Holy Ghost said, 'Separate

for Me Barnabas and Saul for the work I have
called them to do'" (Acts 13:1a,2).

There is much to be gleaned from this passage of
Scripture. The first thing that strikes us is that the
prophets and teachers were gathered together to
minister to the Lord. How seldom we see this today! In
the first place, prophets and teachers are rarely able to
get together regarding anything. The prophet thinks
the teacher is too intellectual, and the teacher thinks
the prophet is too ethereal. The prophet favors
inspiration and revelation, while the teacher favors
illumination and study. The two seem to naturally be at
odds, and this is probably necessary to keep everyone
balanced. The prophet needs the teacher, and the
teacher needs the prophet.

But here we see that everyone has come together,
not to have a prophet's and teacher's conference, but to
minister to the Lord. They have not lost their first love!
Prophetic things have their place, but there is a time
when prophetic things must be put on hold. Teaching
and instruction have their place, but there is a time
when no one should be teaching or saying anything.
There is a time when the saints should gather together
for the purpose of ministering to the Lord.

The Greek word for "ministered" here is *leitourgeo*,
and we get our English word *liturgy* from it. It meant
the performance of priestly or ministerial functions.
Interestingly enough, it could only be used in
connection with the Temple, since that was the only
valid place a priest or minister could perform the
functions. In Acts 13 we see the word used to describe

the Ekklesia in Antioch. What does this mean? Simply this: we are the temple of the living God, a house of living stones, offering up ourselves as the sacrifices, ministering to the Lord as a holy nation, as a royal priesthood. Hence, we need no earthly temple or priest to represent us to God. We worship God in Spirit and in Truth.

The fact that the Holy Spirit moved and revealed the Lord's Need while they were ministering to the Lord is significant. How can we know the Lord's Need unless we have ministered to Him? Perhaps there were a dozen or so missions that might be done, and they could have fulfilled any number of needs and been considered good Christians. But the issue is not how many needs can we meet, but is the Lord's Need met? What if we meet everyone's need but the Lord's Need is not satisfied?

Let us meet the Lord's Need first, and give Him His portion; then we are fit to stand before people and minister to them. This is the motivation for ministering to the Lord. People with no patience for these things will forge ahead on their own, see a need, and move at once to meet it, just like a good business person will do. But the Kingdom is not based on business principles. Our foremost concern is satisfying the Lord's heart, being with Him, meeting His Need. Ministry to men is founded upon ministry to the Lord.

Women Who Ministered to Jesus

> "...Mary Magdalene... Joanna... Susanna, and many others, which ministered to Him of their substance" (Lk. 8:2,3ff).

When the saints are gathered together, wherever such gathering may take place, there are two types of people represented. One type is there to receive, and the other type is there to give. Most people attend a meeting to receive something – a prophetic word, some encouragement, fellowship (e.g., social interaction with spiritual overtones), teaching, the laying on of hands, etc. This explains why meetings can be so dead and lifeless. Everyone is there to receive, and few are there to give. Hence, there is little Life.

But we have learned there is an additional thing to be noted when the saints are gathered together, and that is this: most of the receiving, and what little giving is done, is performed on a horizontal level. In other words, most are coming to receive, a handful are coming to give, but it is still, by and large, focused on meeting man's need. There is little vertical expression towards God, and what little vertical expression there is centers mainly around receiving. We may give Him some praise or some worship or make some prayer requests – we might even ask Him to bless our time together – but for the most part we have not penetrated any higher than the top of our heads.

Praise, worship, and prayer may be part of the meeting for tradition's sake, but they are largely perfunctory, with no more spiritual import than reading the announcements. The meeting is, generally speaking, all about us. We are not saying man's needs should not be met in a meeting; we are saying that meeting man's needs ought not to be the highest aspiration we have when meeting together.

Without a doubt, Jesus wants to minister to you and to meet your needs. His earthly ministry demonstrated His desire to shepherd the sheep, to heal their diseases, and to bring them joy. We should never minimize that. But we should not overemphasize it either. When it came time to die on the cross, what happened to all those people who were healed and delivered and filled with joy by His presence? People will run to the altar when they have a need, then will disappear for six months – until they have another need, and there they are again, crying out to God as before. How quickly we fall away when we are trusting in the Lord for things.

It is clear from the Scriptures that there are two kinds of adoration. There is a mass of people waiting for Jesus to come and minister to *them*, and there is a smaller group of people who have devoted themselves to minister to *Him*. We are not suggesting that it must be either one or the other, but we are definitely saying it should be both, and of the two, ministry to Him is the more important one. Perhaps it is acceptable to begin by seeking the Lord for what the Lord has, but we will never have a strong foundation if that is the only depth we know, and if we remain there for too long it demonstrates an immaturity in our relationship with God.

Intelligent Worship, or Thoughtless Habit?

> "I beg you brothers, by God's mercy, to give up your bodies as a living sacrifice that is holy and well-pleasing to God, for that is your reasonable service" (Rom. 12:1).

Since the Lord Jesus has completed His earthly ministry, we cannot minister to Him "of our substance" as Mary, Joanna, and Susanna did. It is not money, food, clothing, or shelter that He wants from us. So how do we minister to the Lord today? Paul said that as a nation of priests, we are to offer up our own selves as living sacrifices. God does not want our things, and in a very real sense He does not want our works. The Lord wants *us*. If He has *us*, does He not possess all our things and all our works? An alternative rendering of the verse above, instead of *reasonable service* is *intelligent worship.* This is so important that I believe I must quote from Spiros Zodhiates on the word "reasonable," which is translated from *logikos* (logical):

> "In Romans 12:1 the reasonable service or worship is to be understood as the service to God which implies intelligent meditation or reflection without the heathen practices intimated in 1 Corinthians 12:2 and without the Old Testament cultic worship which had become mere thoughtless habit."

In other words, "Spirit and Truth" worship permeates the Ekklesia that Jesus is building and characterizes the relationship that He longs to have with us. "Thoughtless habit" better describes much of what we see in Churchianity. Over 150 years ago, Soren Kierkegaard wrote: "By ceasing to take part in the public worship of God, as it now is (with the claim that it is the Christianity of the New Testament), thou hast constantly one guilt the less, and that a great one: thou dost not take part in treating God as a fool." How much more is this true today?

I seldom quote from others, so I think the point should be made that those who truly see these things have learned them in the crucible of their own experience, and not because they read about it somewhere. We do not need a Greek theologian or a Danish philosopher to tell us what we already know: they simply confirm what has already cut us to the heart.

What do we do about this? Is there anything that can be done? Thankfully, God is raising up more "Acts 13" believers who are determined to minister to the Lord. In addition to the living examples of those who sought to meet the Lord's Need, there is a prophetic and historical precedent for what we are sharing. As we move into the next chapter, we will examine this precedent and demonstrate its applicability to us today. May the Lord quicken this message to all who hunger and thirst for Him.

Chapter Four

When You Pray

"And when you pray, do not be like the hypocrites... but when you pray, enter into your closet and pray in secret... and when you pray, do not use vain repetitions... after this manner therefore, pray..." (Mt. 6:5-9ff).

For too long we have practiced and preached prayer as a means towards our own ends. I am thinking of several popular teachings and books on the market today that make prayer out to be a ritual through which we can induce God to give us whatever we want. This philosophy gives us the illusion of a manageable deity, a "god" who is under our control, having no choice but to respond to a prayer properly worded or recited. A person of average intelligence should be able to see that this is a ridiculous caricature of God – it is a misrepresentation and a deception. The widespread popularity and success of these teachings should make us at least a little suspicious as to the spirit which prompts men to perpetuate it. It cannot be the Holy Spirit.

Jesus takes it for granted that His disciples will pray. This is why four times in a row He says, "*When* you pray" and not "*If* you pray." But from these brief excerpts of Scripture we learn that there are at least two classes of prayer. One is unacceptable to God, and the other is well-pleasing to Him. One is from hypocrites, the other is from a pure heart. One is done openly to be seen by men, the other is hidden to be seen by God alone. One is nothing more than vain repetition to accomplish my own ends, and the other accomplishes God's purpose.

Now, if we pray the prayer of the hypocrite we are wasting our time. God will not respond, He will not move, He will not listen to such praying. That is not to say that someone (something?) will not answer this self-centered prayer: but the answer, when and if it comes, will not come from the Father in heaven. Much praying is done in vain because the one praying has never gone to the Word to investigate the kind of prayer that is well-pleasing to God. Just as there is a worship that is "spirit-and-truth" and there is a worship that is fleshly and vain, so there is a "spirit-and-truth" sort of praying and a flesh-and-blood praying that is done in vanity.

So by the grace of God we would like to look to the Lord to teach us to pray. Let us ask Him to show us the sort of praying that is acceptable to Him.

How NOT to Pray

> "And when you pray, do not be like the hypocrites, for they love to pray standing in the synagogues and on the street corners that they may be seen by

men. I tell you the truth, they have already received
their reward" (Mt. 6:5).

What makes a prayer hypocritical? It is a prayer that is
done in public to be seen by men. It is an outward show
to make one appear spiritual to others. It calls attention
to one's self through loud volume, lengthy discourse, or
spiritual-sounding vocabulary. It is primarily done for
ceremonial benefit only, for the listening ear of men,
and not for God. We want to be seen and heard and
observed. We wish to be known as "prayer warriors" so
we prefer to do our praying in public, by the altar, in
church, or at the prayer meeting, so everyone can see
us. We would have people know us as watchmen,
prophets, and intercessors. But what matters most is
not how people perceive us, but how we truly are before
God.

Hypocrites typically use public praying to preach or
make demands upon others. I was in a meeting once
when a newcomer was asked to pray. Before long he
began talking about his financial needs as if he were
talking to the Lord, but it should have been obvious
that he was merely letting it be known to all present
that he expected a monetary gift. He even said, "I pray
that someone will give me the money I need." And of
course, after the meeting, someone did. But neither the
one who prayed, nor the one who "answered" his
prayer, were in the Spirit. This man should have been
rebuked, but no one rose to the occasion, including
myself. So we all missed the Spirit, but we learned a
lesson. And we never heard from the man again.

Preachers are equally guilty of hypocritical long-windedness. It is interesting to observe how differently someone prays when standing upon a platform before others compared to how they pray in other places. They seem to believe that the spotlight calls for certain words and phrases to be used that they would not otherwise use. This, too, is done for the benefit of the listeners. "Oh, he can pray such powerful prayers!" they exclaim. But this does not mean they are necessarily powerful with God.

Particularly in a day when prayer meetings, prayer gatherings, prayer retreats, and prayer warfare is being emphasized, it is important to understand what the Lord is looking for so we do not fall into a trap of vanity. The experience of many saints seems to indicate that the more we pray in private, the less we will pray in public. The words will be fewer, but they will be far more weighty and valuable. One brother was so broken before God privately that whenever he stepped into the pulpit to pray publicly, all he could do was fall over the lectern and weep, "Oh God!" That is the proper spirit, and how I wish we had more of this kind of prayer.

> "But when you pray, enter into your closet, and after you have shut the door, pray to your Father in secret; and your Father, Who sees what is done secretly, will reward you openly" (Mt. 6:6).

Why does the Lord prefer secret prayer over prayer done in the synagogue (or in the church building)? Prayer that is most valuable to God is done in secret, in the prayer closet, in the inner chamber where no man's eyes can see and no man's ears can hear what is said and done. Thus, everything said and done in secret is for the Lord's sake. Most public praying is done to be seen of men; hence, it has virtually no worth. An abundance of public prayer cannot make up for a lack of secret prayer.

As a child I took this Scripture literally. I would go into a closet and close the door, praying to the Lord in secret. When I got older I would climb to the top of a tree to pray and read. Or I would sneak out while it was still dark so I could pray. As I look back on my life these are the sweetest times of prayer and communion I have ever experienced.

It does not matter whether your closet is a literal closet or not. The issue is the sort of prayer that is offered, whether it is done to be seen by men or if it is done to be seen by God. If we are praying to the Lord for the Lord's sake then we will want to keep holy things holy, private things private, and sacred things sacred. We will not easily repeat to others the intimate details of these encounters with God. It would seem almost sacrilegious to do so.

Is prayer and worship a lifestyle, or is it an event? If it is an event, if most of our praying is done once a week when we gather together, then we will be lacking spiritually. We will sense this lack when we try to flip a switch and become "spiritual enough" to pray. But our corporate prayers have their basis in our secret prayers. The real value is not what is seen outwardly, but what we are inwardly, beneath the surface, as we minister to the Lord in secret.

> "But when you pray, do not use vain repetitions as the heathen do: for they think they will be heard for their much speaking" (Mt. 6:7).

The Greek word for "vain" here is interesting. It comes from the base of another word which means "to handle or squeeze" and implies manipulation, as someone would manipulate clay to make it into something like a bowl or a vase. It is used by Jesus in another context:

> "You hypocrites, well did Isaiah prophesy of you, saying, 'These people draw near to Me with their mouth, and honor Me with their lips, but their hearts are far from Me, for in vain do they worship Me, teaching as doctrines the commandments of men'" (Mt. 15:7-9, ESV).

There is such a thing as vain prayer and vain worship. There is such a thing as a sacrifice acceptable to God and a sacrifice unacceptable to God (see the story of Cain and Abel in Genesis 4). We know exactly what God seeks, and that is, "Spirit and Truth." We also know what He considers to be vanity, manipulation, a waste of time, and self-centered. Vanity includes drawing near to Him with our mouth and honoring Him with our lips while our heart is far from Him. It includes teaching the things of man as if they were the things of God. It includes repeating the same prayers over and over again with a view towards manipulating God. It includes 95% of all that is said and done in a typical church service on Sunday morning. Continually asking God to bless our unacceptable worship every single week is an example of vanity. "In vain do they worship Me."

It may come as a shock and a surprise to most people to learn that much of what they are doing, even the spiritual things (especially the spiritual things), are vanity. People have been taught that so long as they attend church and pray the right prayers for protection, blessings, power or anointing, then everything will be well with them. People who relate to God in this way are behaving like heathens – Jesus says so. Heathen people are not irreligious. They worship! They pray! Hypocrites give! Hypocrites fast! Hypocrites do mighty works in the Name of Jesus! But according to Jesus, it counts for nothing. It is all in vain. They do not really *know* Him, and He does not "know" them either.

> "Do not be like [the heathen], for your Father knows the things you need before you ask Him" (Mt. 6:8).

Here is something interesting! Jesus says not to pray as if we would be heard for our many words or grandiose speech, because the Father knows what we need before we ask Him. Well then! What is the point of praying? If God knows what I need before I ask, why ask at all? If prayer is nothing more than making my needs known to God then perhaps we can stop praying, since He already knows what they are. But perhaps prayer, as Jesus teaches it, has very little to do with making requests to the Lord for my own needs to be met. If so, then to continue praying on the basis of my needs is vanity. Vanity is not only futility, but it is self-centeredness. Thus, "Do not be like the heathen, who vainly repeat the same prayers with a view towards getting their own needs met."

Jesus does not say that since the Father knows what we need, we do not *have* to pray – but if He already knows what we need then it should definitely change the *way* we pray. When we do pray we should not behave like a hypocrite or a heathen, obsessed with ourselves. Our needs are already known to the Lord. So it is not as though we have to go to God and inform Him as to the details of our situation in order to fully appraise Him of what is happening. We might give our doctor such detailed information so a proper diagnosis can be made, but the Lord does not need any assistance from us in order to help Him figure out the problem. Nor does He need us to tell Him what needs to be done, as if we know what is called for and He does not.

What if prayer is something deeper than rehearsing my needs to the Lord? What if prayer is a means toward a higher end than getting my circumstances and my surroundings in order? In other words, what if prayer is not about my needs, my desires, my wants, my requests, or my situation at all? What if prayer is meant to meet the *Lord's* need? What if, instead of coming to the Lord with *our* expectation as to the outcome, we come to the Lord, interested in knowing what *His* expectation is? What if prayer is not about giving voice to *my* will at all, but is about giving voice to *His* will?

This concept may be too radical for some, because it will require a further death to their Self. But since the Father knows what we have need of before we ask, prayer must not be primarily concerned with telling Him what He already knows. Since we are to pray, and since the Lord knows our needs already, does this not indicate a higher calling and a deeper work to be done in prayer than merely voicing my personal prayer requests? To the heathen and the hypocrite, who are so absorbed with Self, vanity (futility and self-centeredness) is evident everywhere, and in their praying in particular. According to the Scriptures, it appears that Jesus is bringing us to a deeper understanding of prayer. So after what manner *should* we pray then? Jesus makes it very plain.

How to Pray

> "Pray after this manner: 'Our Father in heaven, may Your Name be hallowed, may Your Kingdom come, may Your Will be done: as in heaven, so in earth'" (Mt. 6:9,10).

Now that we know the kind of prayer that is not acceptable to the Lord, it is time for us to look at the kind of prayer that is acceptable. The Lord Jesus is not giving us a prayer to repeat word for word, for that would be contrary to everything He has told us up to this point (observe how we still cling to it ritualistically anyway). Instead, He gives us a pattern, a prototype, a foundation for all prayer by saying, "Pray after this manner," or, "Pray along these lines."

At once we are lifted up from the earthly situation and are made to focus upon a heavenly Father, a heavenly Kingdom, and a heavenly Will. I believe it is so important for us to see this. Prayer does not begin on the earth, it begins in the heavens. It does not begin with man, it begins with the Father. It does not begin with man's need, but with God's will. Our praying is ineffectual because we pray as earthly men with an earthly perspective concerning earthly things. See how far and above this manner of praying is when compared to the hypocrite praying in public to be seen of men! Prayer ought to bring us up into the heavenlies, not bring us down deeper into the earth. It ought to focus our vision on the Father, not on man, or the problems of man. Spiritual prayer begins in the Spirit; heavenly prayer begins in the heavenlies.

When we pray "after this manner" we are transported and elevated beyond flesh-and-blood, beyond the natural, beyond the earthly, beyond the seen-and-felt universe in which we live. We are at once brought into alignment with Someone larger than ourselves, Someone higher, Someone greater. This Someone has an agenda, and is working all things together in one accord towards this agenda. What is the agenda? It is the Will and the Kingdom. So what is the Will and the Kingdom? The Will is "all things in Christ" and the Kingdom is the fulfillment of that Will, when Christ has the preeminence. All of God's movements are towards this End.

So the chief objective of prayer is to bring us into cooperation with the Father so that we are harmonious with Him – with respect to our love relationship as well as our working relationship. Much time and effort in prayer is spent trying to get God involved with *our* agenda, with *our* plans, with *our* goals, with *our* cause, with *our* needs, real or imagined. But after all, who is the Master? Who is the servant? Whose will are we seeking anyway: ours, or His? If we have not touched upon the Will and the Kingdom in our praying then we are praying in vain, because God cannot contradict Himself, and cannot answer such prayer. If our agenda is not harmonious with His then our agenda has to go. Most of our prayers are simply too small, too narrow-minded, and too constricted. We do not see anything beyond our present surroundings. We have not seen the big picture. We do not have a heavenly perspective. So to begin with we must empty ourselves of all preconceived ideas and seek the Lord's Will and the Lord's Kingdom when we pray, for this truly consecrates the Father in prayer.

> "Give us today's bread again as usual; and as we have forgiven others their sins, so forgive us our sins" (Mt. 6:11,12).

The Lord does not tell us *not* to make our requests known to Him. It is appropriate to thankfully acknowledge Him on a daily basis as our Provider and the One Who forgives. The difference is this: when we pray the Will and the Kingdom, when we lose ourselves and our agenda, when we come to the Lord to meet His need, then we will find our needs are met; but even if they are not met, we will not care. Our desire is for Him, and so long as we are in His Will and in His Kingdom, the issue of whether or not my personal needs are met becomes of secondary importance. Prayer is not the vehicle whereby I get my needs met. It is the means through which God's Need is met. Now that I am praying on behalf of God's Will and God's Kingdom, now that I am praying in alignment with God's desire for the ages, He will be sure to supply me with what I need (indeed, nothing can prevent it, for nothing has been able to prevent it for billions of years). As I have sought first the Kingdom, all that is required will be added to me. Not for my sake, you see, but for His sake. As I have vested myself into His Kingdom, He has vested Himself into my well-being. How could it be otherwise?

For after all, where is the Kingdom? Here, or there, in the future, in the past? No, the Kingdom is within you (Lk. 17:21). When we pray God's Will and God's Kingdom, are we not asking for Christ to increase and for us to decrease? Are we not asking for Christ to have the greater preeminence in us individually as disciples? For the moment, forget about bringing people together or getting everyone to see the same thing. If each of us prayed this with no greater goal but for ourselves, would this not by extension include the entire Ekklesia, of which we are members? So we are praying for Christ to have the preeminence in us individually as disciples; in the Ekklesia corporately; and in all of creation collectively. We are aligning ourselves with some very powerful forces, all working together towards God's Ultimate Purpose.

Now whether or not you consider the bread to be physical or spiritual (or both), it is provided daily. And, on a daily basis, forgiveness of sins is provided. Bread speaks of our Life, and forgiveness of sins speaks of our walk. Daily we require Life in order to live. Daily we offend others, and daily we offend God. So daily we have need of forgiveness. Quite frankly, whatever else we may think we need is summed up into these two things. Everything else is good to have, and God may be pleased to grant them, but they are not absolutely necessary. No one has a Scriptural "right" to make demands upon the Father for whatever they want, no more than my children should expect me to give them everything they ask for.

Since we are already blessed with every spiritual blessing in Christ (Eph. 1:3), the bulk of our prayers ought to be centered on God's Will and not our wants *unless* – and here is where it gets interesting and powerful – *unless* what *we* want is what *He* wants. God will deny no prayer that is in agreement with what He Himself wants to do. In fact, He is the One Who makes His Will known to us so we can voice our agreement to it in prayer, so it will come to pass. Conformity to Christ includes wanting what He wants, and if this is taking place in us, the first place it will manifest itself is in our praying, for this is where the exchange of His Life for my life is taking place. And by now we should already know that God only wants *One Thing*. Eventually, that is all we will want, and that is all we will be able to pray. The easiest way to get your wants met in prayer is to only want *One Thing*.

> "Lead us not into temptation, but deliver us from evil: for the Kingdom is Yours, the Power is Yours, and the Glory is Yours. May it be so forever" (Mt. 6:13).

As we begin with the Kingdom, so we end with the Kingdom. On what basis may we claim deliverance from evil? On the basis that the Kingdom is of God, the Power is of God, and the Glory is of God.

What is evil? All that is of Antichrist is evil. Antichrist resists God's movement towards Christ as All in All. Whether or not this culminates in a last day dictator is beside the point. Antichrist has been with us from the beginning. The spirit of Antichrist has always resisted the preeminence of Christ, from Lucifer's rebellion to the sins of your flesh. A thing does not have to be bad to be evil. It could be like an angel of light. Of course, bad things are evil, but even seemingly good things are evil if they are not bringing us further into Christ as All in All. So if God's Highest Good is Christ, then anything less than Christ or apart from Christ is evil.

So many are under the impression that the devil has a kingdom, but Scripture does not support this. "Thine is the Kingdom." The Kingdom belongs to God. God never gave anything to the devil. Even in the Old Testament, before Jesus walked the earth, it is said, "The earth is the *Lord's*, and the fullness thereof: the world, and they that dwell therein" (Ps. 24:1). Again, many are obsessed with the alleged "power" of darkness, and anyone who has the ability to deceive another has the ability to control them, but here we are told "Thine is the Power." There is no intrinsic power of darkness, there is only power over individuals gained through deception. The True Power is not held by darkness, but by God, through Jesus Christ, in heaven as well as in earth (Mt. 28:18). Finally, "Thine is the Glory." It is this Glory of Christ as He in fact is that manifests to us by revelation, and this Glory is indeed manifested in the heavens as well as in the whole earth (Ps. 8).

Now if we carefully look at these three items – the Kingdom, the Power, and the Glory – we see that it is as much for earth as it is for heaven. It truly represents all that "as in heaven, so in earth" means. Yet there is, on the earth, something that seems to challenge the preeminence of Christ, as if to say that there is another Kingdom, another Power, and another Glory, whether it be of men or of satan (Lk. 4:5,6). To pray in this manner is to declare otherwise. It is to stand upon the earth and give testimony that there is only One Kingdom, One Power, and One Glory, and these belong to the Father and to His Christ. Of course, we must see this and believe it in order to pray it. But this, essentially, is the Testimony of Jesus and the ministry of the overcomers.

The thing which hampers our praying the most is the smallness of our vision. Prayer is only a means to an End, and the End is to see Christ established as the Preeminent One on the earth just like in heaven. Prayer aligns us with the heart of God so that we only desire the One Thing that He desires.

We cannot, we should not, have faith in prayer itself. How easy it is to put our confidence in a method or a technique for praying and begin relating to God like a heathen. How easy it is to put our confidence in man and begin relating to God like a hypocrite. It is interesting to see that as powerful as "the Lord's Prayer" is, it is nevertheless done behind closed doors, and in secret. We are not told that we must go to strategic points on the globe in order to exercise our authority. We are not given the names of demons or principalities with which we must engage ourselves. Not at all. In our prayer closet, once the door is shut, we merely pray in this manner to the Father, and He will reward us openly.

And lest we forget, Christ is our reward. We seek not His things, but Him. We seek not our Kingdom, but His. We rely not in our power, but in His. And as we are decreased, He is increased, and His glory is revealed and made manifest in us and through us. This is true prayer, provided we are willing to leave our ground and come onto His ground, praying His Will and not ours.

O Father, reveal Your Son in us. Teach us to pray. Your Name be sanctified. We stand for your Kingdom and for Your Will in the earth. May Your Kingdom come – in us. May Your Will be done – in us. As in heaven, so in earth. We thank you that as we seek first Your Kingdom, everything we need is provided. Deliver us from all that is Antichrist, from all that is natural, from all that is flesh-and-blood, from all that is carnal, from all that is earthly, and establish us in the Kingdom of Your Dear Son. We recognize no kingdom but Yours, no power but Yours, no glory but Yours. May it be so forever. Amen.

Chapter Five

When You Fast

"But when you fast, anoint your head and wash your face, so that your fasting is not evident to others, but is evident to your Father who sees everything which is done secretly; and your Father, who sees what you do secretly, will reward you openly" (Mt. 6:18).

We have sensed a need for some clear teaching along the lines of prayer and fasting, and of the two, fasting seems to be the most misunderstood or the least talked about among Christians. Those in the Western world have very little experience with fasting, whereas those in the Eastern world are very experienced. Fasting is not limited to Christians only; most religious people in the East observe some kind of fasting, regardless of their faith.

That Jesus intends for His disciples to fast is made clear by the words, "When you fast..." If it were a matter of personal preference the Lord would have said, "*If* you fast." The word *when* implies that there will be times when a disciple of the Lord is called into a time of fasting. It seems to be a foregone conclusion. Fasting is as much a part of a disciple's life as prayer; hence the Lord couples, "When you pray" with "when you fast" in His teaching to the disciples.

We can account for the lack of specific direction in the Bible about *how* to fast by reiterating again that fasting was, and is, commonly practiced in the East, and people knew how to do it. Some practical advice along these lines may be helpful to those who are not as experienced but sense the Lord is quickening them to seek His face with prayer and with fasting.

First, let us establish the history of fasting in the Bible and its validity for the Church today.

Biblical Examples of Fasting

The most notable examples of fasting are found in the lives of the prophets. The prophetic ministry is inescapably linked to fasting. Moses fasted for forty days on two separate occasions (Deut. 9:9,19). Elijah fasted for forty days in the wilderness (1 Ki. 19:8). Jesus also fasted for forty days (Lk. 4:2). Daniel fasted on several occasions, and he gives us the most insight into different ways to fast (Dan. 1:8; 9:3; 10:2,3). Esther asked the Jews to fast for her by going without food or drink for three days (Est. 4:16). David frequently fasted as a way to show sorrow for his sins (2 Sam. 12:16-20; 69:10; 109:24). Ezra and Nehemiah were both men of fasting and prayer (Ezr. 8:21; Neh. 1:4). The Jews observed regular fasts as part of the Law of Moses, and fasting seemed to be the rallying cry for all Israel whenever a time of great crisis was at hand (Joel 1:13,14).

Even wicked king Ahab was granted some grace from God because he humbled himself with prayer and fasting (1 Ki. 21:25-29). So fasting is not limited to saints and holy people. Nineveh was the capital of Assyria, one of the first world powers, and a pagan society. Yet when Jonah preached that Nineveh would be destroyed in forty days, the response was uncharacteristic and surprising:

> "...the people of Nineveh believed God, and proclaimed a fast, and put on sackcloth, from the greatest of them even to the least of them. For word came unto the king of Nineveh, and he arose from his throne, and he laid his robe from him, and covered him with sackcloth, and sat in ashes. And he caused it to be proclaimed and published through Nineveh by saying, 'Let neither man nor beast, herd nor flock, taste any thing: let them not feed, nor drink water: But let man and beast be covered with sackcloth, and cry mightily unto God: yea, let them turn every one from his evil way, and from the violence that is in their hands. Who can tell if God will turn and repent, and turn away from His fierce anger, that we perish not?' And God saw their works, that they turned from their evil way; and God repented of the evil, that He had said that He would do unto them and He did it not" (Jon. 3:5-10).

It is noteworthy that the Assyrians would not even allow their animals to eat or drink during this time of national repentance. We have yet to see the likes of this anywhere else in the world.

Fasting is not limited to the Old Testament. Scripture tells us that Anna never departed from the Temple, but ministered to the Lord with prayer and fasting day and night (Lk. 2:37). John the Baptist and his disciples observed fasting, as did the Pharisees (Mt. 9:14). Jesus indicated that once He returned to heaven, His disciples would fast as well (Mt. 9:15).

And so they did. Because Cornelius fasted and prayed, the Gospel was first preached to the Gentiles in his home, establishing that Christ was not the Savior for Jews only, but for the whole world (Acts 10:30). Fasting and prayer launched the first missionary journey of Paul that would turn the whole world upside down (Acts 13:2,3). The apostles fasted and prayed each time they confirmed elders (Acts 14:23). Paul recommended that husbands and wives occasionally abstain from sexual relations, by consent, for the purpose of fasting and prayer (1 Cor. 7:5). He fasted often himself (2 Cor. 6:5; 11:27).

The Purpose of Fasting

If we will take the time to read through the Scriptures cited above we will find four primary reasons for fasting. It is time to fast when:

1. We want to minister to the Lord (*Anna, the believers in Antioch*);

2. We want to show personal contrition and sorrow for our sins (*David, Nineveh, Ahab*) or for the sins of others (*Daniel, Nehemiah, Ezra*);

3. We need revelation concerning the present and direction concerning the future (*Daniel, Cornelius, the apostles*);

4. We experience times of great spiritual crisis and conflict (*Jesus, Moses, Elijah, Daniel, Esther, Paul*).

Our study of the examples above also show four kinds of fasting. They include:

1. *The Supernatural Fast* – going beyond the limits of human endurance by the direct hand of God, such as Moses' forty day fast in which he did not eat or drink. Humanly speaking, a man cannot survive without water for longer than three or four days. This was a supernatural fast, and is not likely to be repeated.

2. *The Total Fast* – going without food or water, such as Esther's fast and Nineveh's fast. Desperate times call for desperate measures, and the pending destruction of an entire nation or city would call for this kind of fast. It should never be attempted for

longer than three days, and only if the Lord's direction is unmistakably clear.

3. *The Normal Fast* – going without food, but drinking liquids. This is the traditional and most common form of fasting, and is the kind of fast Jesus observed in the wilderness. We know this because the Bible says He was hungry, but it does not say He was thirsty (Lk. 4:2). A normal fast will be of varying length, anywhere from one meal, to one day, three days, seven days, or even twenty-one days, but it will never exceed forty days.

4. *The Partial Fast* – observing a special diet, but not necessarily abstaining from all food. Daniel was a master of this particular kind of fast, and it is preferable for those who cannot totally go without food for health or other reasons. Daniel observed this kind of fast when he refused meat and wine and asked for pulse (a kind of vegetable stew) and water. On another occasion he observed the same fast and also abstained from "pleasant bread," which may have been something like cake or some delicacy. It is a known fact that Charles Wesley fasted by eating only bread and water. A partial fast may also include going without breakfast for several days in succession, or eating only one meal a day. The possibilities for this kind of fast are

endless, and it is a good place for the novice to begin.

Preparing to Fast

It is better to live a life of continual fasting and prayer than it is to suddenly find yourself in a situation which calls for fasting and be totally unprepared to deny yourself. We can and should live, eat, and drink modestly at all times. If we are used to eating all we want then it will be very difficult to respond to the Lord when He desires us to seek His face with fasting. So we should be on the alert, constantly watching and praying, so that we are ready to respond immediately to the circumstances that are presented to us. It may be that we have no time to prepare at all, but the situation is so urgent that we drop everything immediately when a word like Jonah's is brought to our attention. We should conduct ourselves in such a manner that we are ready at a moment's notice should the Lord require us.

Then again, you may sense that the Lord is calling you to fast and pray but the timing is left up to you as to when to begin. Suppose, for instance, that the Lord lays upon my heart that I should make preparations to fast and pray. As I respond to this leading I will want to seek direction from the Lord as to what kind of fast to observe and the duration of it. The longer and more intense the kind of fast we are led to observe, the more we should prepare. I will want to arrange my schedule accordingly so as to allow for extra time in prayer. I will also want to begin eating less in anticipation of the fast. This will make the transition easier. To gorge oneself the day before the fast defeats the purpose. I will also want to make my wife aware of my plans so she can schedule things accordingly. Otherwise, it is a secret between myself and the Lord. So these are some of the things to be considered.

In addition, if you are pregnant, or have a medical condition such as diabetes or an eating disorder, it would be wise to consult your doctor before undertaking any kind of change in diet. It would be appropriate to tell your doctor that you want to fast for religious purposes and ask for his or her advice before commencing.

The body adjusts to fasting by degrees. For that reason, it is foolish to begin with a forty day fast if you have never even fasted longer than one day. It is better to begin slowly. As you are faithful with a few small fasts, larger fasts will come. Since our praying and fasting is to be done in secret, there is nothing to be gained by attempting a long fast for which we are spiritually and physically unprepared.

There should be some clear indication or reason why you are fasting. We are not commanded to observe certain days or months in which we are to fast. So the only valid reason to initiate a fast is when one senses the leading of the Lord to do so in response to one of the four situations listed previously. There are medicinal benefits of fasting, but I would say that if you are fasting for medicinal benefits or for weight-loss then you are not fasting unto the Lord. We are out to benefit His Kingdom, not ourselves. Thus, we should know the purpose of our fast before we begin so that our prayers and intercessions will be centered around that purpose. We are not trying to put the Lord into a box, but we do stress that a definite aim and a particular outcome should be expected. We cannot fast until the whole world is saved: this is neither definite, nor is it reasonable. We cannot even fast until a particular person is saved, let alone a nation, because we cannot control other people with our prayers. Fasting will not change God, and it will not change others, but it will change *us*. So, we may fast for specific answers to prayer, such as revelation, direction, forgiveness of sins, etc. We need specificity in order to gauge the effectiveness of our efforts. Once we have the answer we seek, our fasting has served its purpose.

While You Are Fasting

There are huge blocks of time that become available to those who fast. We are able to redeem several minutes, sometimes hours a day, when we do not eat. In the first place, much time is spent thinking about food, shopping for food, preparing meals, eating them, and cleaning up afterwards. If we fast from three meals we can usually invest two or three hours of extra time into prayer, or study of the Word. This time is most valuable when fasting, and should not be squandered.

In addition, the body does not require as much sleep when fasting as it does when eating. After a couple of days the digestive system begins to rest, and with less bodily function there is less need for sleep. We may find five hours of sleep will do just as well for us when fasting, as seven hours will do when eating. Insomnia is common while one is fasting, and for this we should be thankful, because it allows us even more time for prayer and seeking God's face.

There are some physical side effects that will present themselves early on. These vary according to the kind of fast being observed. People with jobs to attend and families to care for should consider a partial fast, drinking fruit and vegetable juices but abstaining from food. This not only provides the body with the vitamins that it needs for you to continue your activities, but it reduces the dizziness and weakness some people feel when drinking only water.

Regardless of the kind of fast you observe, it is normal to feel hungry, to experience some dizziness and lack of energy, and to have a headache. These symptoms are temporary and will become less pronounced after the first day. This is due in part to the stored-up toxins that are being released through the body, and eventually you will feel much better. Just remember to move slowly when sitting or rising. Eventually all feelings of hunger leave, and one feels that they could go without food forever! Fasting is a natural purgative for body as well as soul.

You will also notice a reduced libido during your time of fasting. This is to be expected, as food is closely related to sex drive. This is why Paul stressed the importance of one spouse fasting with the consent and cooperation of the other. Those who are unequally yoked need to be especially led of the Lord in these matters.

Spiritually speaking there are side effects as well. There is a greater awareness of spiritual things, and we might add, things we may become aware of while fasting are not always from the Holy Spirit. One should not fear these things, but as usual, should test all things, and hold fast to what is true. Do not assume that every voice, impression, dream, or vision experienced while fasting is necessarily from God. To do so is to invite serious error. We should wait on the Lord, and as always, not live according to our feelings.

While fasting it is important to be discreet and properly motivated. The Bible has a lot to say about people who fasted for the wrong reasons, and God said He would pay no attention to their fasting (Isa. 58; Jer. 14:12). We do not want to fast in vain, or in order to be seen or approved by man. We do not want to call attention to ourselves. The story is told of a monk who sat down at the dinner table with several others but refused the food when it was served, announcing that he would only have water and a little salt, for he was fasting. The abbot said, "It would have been better for you to go ahead and feast with us than to let this thing be known in the presence of so many."

People will naturally invite you to eat because this is polite. If you are fasting, you can easily say, "No thank you, I'm on a special diet today!" Most people will not want to tempt you to break a diet, and will instinctively stop offering you food. If they want to know what kind of diet it is, tell them it is a liquid diet. Or, you can simply say that you have already eaten; and if you have been feeding on the Word of the Lord during your fast, then this statement is entirely consistent with what Jesus told His disciples: "I have meat to eat that you know not of... My meat is to do His Will" (Jn. 4:32-34).

After the Fast

When the fast is concluded we need to take the same approach as when we began. We should slowly increase our food intake back to its usual amount – or less, if at all possible. The stomach capacity will be diminished, meaning it will not take as much food to fill us. We should take advantage of this and avoid stuffing ourselves. The next time we fast it will require less physical preparation.

Again, the way we break the fast is determined by the kind of fast we observed and the duration of it. One can resume eating normally after a one or two day fast without complication. For longer fasts, it is better to eat soup the first day, then a little fruit and vegetables the next day, and then some more solid food the third day. Do what seems right, but avoid sitting down to a feast as soon as the fast is complete. It will have a negative impact upon you physically as well as spiritually.

We often take our daily bread for granted. Fasting restores a healthy respect and reverence for God's provision. The first meal after a fast is sacred, and you may want to break the fast by taking communion. We should certainly give thanks to God as we resume eating with a greater appreciation for the food on our plate.

The Need is Great

We especially want to give this teaching to the Body of Christ because the Lord's Need is so great for those who will seek His face with prayer and fasting. There is much more that could be said, but our goal is to provide our brothers and sisters with a practical foundation from which they may begin this holy and necessary work. If during the course of your seeking the Lord you have additional questions or need some practical help in this area, please let us know.

May the Lord strengthen His people as we seek His Will and His Kingdom during these perilous times.

Chapter Six

God's Prophetic Priesthood

"They shall enter into My sanctuary and they shall come near to My table, to minister unto Me, and they shall keep My charge" (Eze. 44:16).

P reviously we established that the Lord has sought to secure for Himself individuals who will enter into a love relationship with Him on an intimate level. We described how the Lord has a "need" for man just as man has a need for the Lord; a void which is only satisfied when the two become one. We also touched upon the general failure of our current system of organized worship to truly satisfy the heart of God, and how the offering up of ourselves as living sacrifices constitutes ministering to the Lord in Spirit and Truth.

We saw that anyone who has ever been close to fulfilling God's desire or satisfying His heart has specialized in ministering to Him. We looked at some individuals whose lives were characterized by the fact that they ministered to the Lord, and we saw that the Lord revealed Himself to them in a mighty way. We even made the statement that apart from an intimate relationship with God, founded upon ministering to the Lord, there can be no revelation, no prophetic sense, and no depth of knowing Him.

If we could sum up everything said thus far, it would read like this: you were created to love Him, and to be loved by Him. It is all about Him, and not about you or your needs. We are not the center of the universe, He is. He was not created for us, we were created for Him. This is the heart of the matter. When the Lord began to draw me even deeper into this ministry to Him, these are the words He spoke to me: "You were created to love Me, you were created to be loved by Me." This is such a holy, personal thing that I am reluctant to share it, but I believe it is an open invitation to everyone, not a special invitation for me alone. Even so, why does God want "me" to minister to Him? Who am I? What can I give the Lord? And how does this relate to everything else I am doing for God? I know what it means to teach and write and pray for people and pastor a church; I can get my hands on that, and I used to think that was quite enough. But this thing of ministering to the Lord is a depth that few know anything about. I know so little about it myself. But I do know this much: there is an ocean of difference between ministering *for* the Lord and ministering *to* the Lord.

There are a handful of people who are being stirred up to minister *to* the Lord. Please understand that *we* are not calling forth a remnant of people who are to be more spiritual than the rest. We are simply acknowledging the fact that although many are called by God, few respond; thus, few are chosen. There is a reason why the sons of Zadok were permitted into the Holy Place to minister to the Lord, while the other

Levites were to remain in the outer court to minister to the people. This is not happenstance. Some, even now, are hearing the call of the Lord and are leaving the outer court, and pressing into the Holy Place to minister to the Lord. We need to understand why. We need to look at the outer court and compare it to the sanctuary. We need to compare the ministry to the people with the ministry to the Lord.

The Lord has shared some of the greatest things with me when I simply asked, "Why?" If we know "what" then we know His Will; but if we know "why" then we know His Ways. His Will is His Desire, His Ways are how He goes about securing His desire. We need to know both if we are to cooperate with Him. So let us examine His Will and His Ways together.

Organized Religion: Primarily Concerned With the Outer Court

> "And the Levites that are gone away far from Me, when Israel went astray, which went astray away from Me after their idols; they shall even bear their iniquity. Yet they shall be ministers in My sanctuary, having charge at the gates of the house, and ministering to the house: they shall slay the burnt offering and the sacrifice for the people, and they shall stand before them to minister unto them" (Eze. 44:10,11).

The vision of Ezekiel's temple is symbolic of the Ekklesia. It is beyond the scope of our study to go through and develop that thought in detail, but I mention it so that we understand there is something here that is applicable to us today. If it is only applicable to the Israelites then it has little relevance to us today, but it is, in fact, highly relevant.

There is an outer court, and there is an inner court. There are those who primarily minister to the people, and there are those who primarily minister to the Lord. To begin with, we must look at the outer court so we can understand the inner court. So what is the outer court? It represents ministry to the people, the offering up of sacrifices. It is visible and public, full of action. Its ministers are in plain view and easily identified. There is much work to be done. Because it is public, everyone has access to it. This is where all the activity is. The Levites stand in the outer court to minister to the people.

But read our text again. Who is serving in this outer court? The Levites who went astray and worshipped idols. Part of "bearing their iniquity" is that they are forbidden from drawing near to the Lord in the inner court. They are forever bound to the outer court, the ministry to the people. They are not permitted to go any deeper. Is this not a tragedy? "They shall not come near unto Me, to do the office of a priest unto Me, nor to come near to any of My holy things, in the most holy place: but they shall bear their shame, and their abominations which they have committed" (v.13).

Here is the greatest single problem with Organized Religion: it cannot bring people any deeper into God than it can go itself. Its people are destined to remain in the outer court. Technically speaking, they are "in the sanctuary," but they are far from God, and cannot draw near to Him. It is better to be out of "church" and "in God" than to be "in church" and "away from God." How nice it would be to have both, but the reality is that God and "church" often contradict one another. Many have come to realize that they have to choose between the two.

The ministers of the outer court are in love with their ministry to the people, with the elements and instruments of the work, and with their status and position in the outer court. They cannot lead us where they are unwilling to go themselves. Of course, I am speaking generally. I think it is wrong to assume that anyone who pastors a church is part of this group. That would be incorrect. We are talking about an inward thing. I am not saying you must leave the outer court in order to obey God. But I will say this: if you are not willing to forsake the ministry of the outer court, then you cannot minister in the inner court. You cannot stand in both courts at the same time.

Ministry to People, or Ministry to the Lord?

> "These people draw near to Me with their mouth, and they honor Me with their lips, but their hearts are far from Me" (Isa. 12a).

Let me get right to the heart of the matter. What is it about Organized Religion that grieves me the most? I think it is this: the impression it gives that there is no inner court at all, that the outer court is all that there is. Everything centers around ministry to the people, and the ministry to the Lord is forgotten, or worse, is done in such a way that it deceives the people into thinking they are ministering to the Lord when they are not.

I wish a pastor could get up in front of the congregation and say, "It is good for us to be here, and it is right for us to fellowship, but you must understand that this is only the outer court. Everything we are doing is for ourselves. We have yet to touch God. There is an inner court in which we stop ministering to one another, and must minister to the Lord. That is where we are going. We cannot be satisfied until the Lord is satisfied." If this is the pastor's heart then praise God for it! But how many pastors have you heard say that? And how many, having said it and begun to practice it, would remain in the pastorate for long?

The ministry of the outer court is important, but we have made it important for the wrong reasons. Instead of seeing it as the means through which we enter the inner court, we have made it the entire focus. We are more interested in "curb appeal," making the outer court look good to visitors and meaningful for those seeking a "worship experience," while the Lord Himself stands in the inner court, forgotten and ignored. How we feel about the service and whether or not we got anything out of it has become more important than whether or not the Lord's Need is met. Can you not see how far we have fallen?

May I say frankly that the Lord *will not* come forth out of the inner court, out of the Holy Place, to meet you in the outer court, no matter how devoted, sincere, or zealous you are. The way is open in Christ, but you must go to Him, and to do so you must pass through the outer court to get to where He is in the inner court.

Now just observe how we do the exact opposite. We gather together in the outer court and pray, shout, sing, worship, and expect the Lord to shower us with His presence or move upon us in a tangible way, i.e., "fall upon us" or "visit us" or "show up." From start to finish this process takes about thirty minutes to an hour, and sure enough, there is some kind of "manifestation" produced so as to make everyone believe that the Lord responded to them. Nonsense! He will not meet you in the shallowness of the outer court once a week for an hour or so at a time convenient to you and your schedule. You must enter the Holy Place of the inner court to draw near to God. The lesser approaches the Greater, not the other way around.

A Personal Experience

It may be helpful to go back to the time in my life when the Lord first began to deal with me about ministering to the Lord. Many people believe I had a falling out with the church, and have developed my particular philosophy since then. Quite the opposite, in fact. The Lord began to deal with me and show me things while I was still very much a part of Churchianity. Eventually, my decision to live according to the Truth caused me to have a falling out with the church. So the falling out was the end result of where the revelation brought me, and not the by-product of having been "hurt" or disillusioned (and I always have to emphasize that one can never have a falling out with the "True Church"- the *Ekklesia*, the Body of Christ - because that is not the same thing as Churchianity).

I was occupying my usual place in the church one Sunday morning, singing and worshipping the Lord, just as I had done for countless Sunday mornings my entire life. Nothing unusual or out of the ordinary was going on. It is difficult to describe what I perceived next, but I can only say that a sense of deep loneliness came over me, a sort of grief. Soon I stopped singing altogether and just listened to those around me. Then I opened my eyes and looked around. I had no reason to feel lonely; I perceived that this sensation was not mine, but the Lord was allowing me to share something that was coming from Him.

I realized that we were singing *about* the Lord, but not *to* the Lord. We were talking *about* the Lord, but not *to* the Lord. We have seen people do this with senior citizens, talking about them as if they were not present, thinking they do not know the difference, while they silently suffer the humility of being treated as if they are not even there. It was then that I understood that we treat the Lord the same way.

It was not as if this was a particularly bad service. I have been in bad services, and this one was pretty good! But that made it even worse. The better "our" service, the more the Lord seemed to be left out. It was like having a birthday party for someone and getting so excited about the food and the drinks and the music and our new clothes and the presents that we did not notice that the person having the birthday is sitting over in the corner, alone. I saw that "our" service really was "ours" – for us, and not for the Lord. The singing, the praying, the preaching, the offering, everything was for us, and *whether the Lord was satisfied or not,* we would be there the next Sunday doing the exact same thing *because it satisfied us.*

I was so affected by what had been revealed to me that I sat down, took out a piece of paper, and wrote down these words so I would not forget that moment: "It is not what *I* need or what *I* want. I have come before You, Lord, to meet *Your* Need, to satisfy *Your* Want, to yield to *Your* Desire. I have not come to *receive* a single thing from You, but rather to *give* all that I have and all that I am."

I still have this piece of paper today. In some small way I felt that the Lord was satisfied with this simple surrender; indeed, satisfied and pleased in a way that could not be equaled with all the singing and praying and giving and preaching that we were doing. According to outward appearances, we were "on fire" and "alive," but I had seen things the way the Lord saw them: "You have a name that you are living, but you are dead" (Rev. 3:1b).

When we see things as God sees them it is a critical moment in our walk with Him. We can easily dismiss the experience and continue on as before. We can argue against it, rationalize it away, or forget about the whole thing. I am convinced that there are hundreds, if not thousands, of people who go through the same experience on Sunday morning but they choose to ignore it. The reality is too painful to deal with, too upsetting to question.

But as I continued to ponder this experience I realized that if what I had seen was true, then much of what I had been doing in the Name of Jesus was a waste of time, was not pleasing to God, was not acceptable to God, and did nothing to meet His Need or satisfy His heart. It did, of course, meet *my* needs and satisfy *my* heart. How wonderful to be in front of the people as they listened to me preach and teach and lead worship! Sunday was the best day of the week, for it was then that everyone could appreciate just what an anointed man of God I really was! They were happy to let me lead them, and I was happy to be their leader, and so everyone was happy. Everyone, it seems, but the Lord, Who called to us from within the inner court while we played "church" in the outer court.

I learned that even something as spiritual-sounding as "wanting His presence" is tainted by the egocentricity of the outer-court worshipper. We want the "presence" so bad that we are willing to manufacture it and give the Lord credit for something which is fleshly and profane. What we really seek is not the "presence," but the "presents." As such, we have lost the ability to discern the difference between God and man, between Spirit and flesh, between holy and common. Every new thing that comes along sweeps us right off our feet, and later we wonder how we could have been so deceived, and why we feel so empty inside. We are chasing fantasies and illusions, meetings and manifestations, not the living God of the inner court.

Those Who Minister to the Lord Maintain the Sanctity of the Inner Court

> "But the priests, the Levites, the sons of Zadok, that kept the charge of My sanctuary when the children of Israel went astray from Me, they shall come near to Me to minister unto Me, and they shall stand before Me to offer unto Me the fat and the blood, saith the Lord God: they shall enter into My sanctuary, and they shall come near to My table, to minister unto Me, and they shall keep My charge" (Eze. 44:15,16).

Now that we have sufficiently identified the ministry of the outer court, we turn our attention to the ministry of the inner court. Keep in mind that this is Ezekiel's temple, not the Tabernacle, and not the Temple of Solomon. It is different from all others. But we are not trying to identify each individual room or item, we are simply taking note of the difference between the outer and the inner. The outer court is comprised of many things, as is the inner court. But we are more interested in the ministry itself, and how the ministry to people is compared to the ministry to the Lord. These two are *not* the same.

What is significant about the sons of Zadok, and how is it applicable to us today? The sons of Zadok were selected to minister to the Lord because they "kept the charge" of the sanctuary when the children of Israel went astray from the Lord and worshipped idols. In plain language it means this: when things began to decline and the temple was defiled, the sons of Zadok decided they would no longer try to keep the outer court sanctified, but they moved into the inner court and continued to minister to the Lord. When the outer court was defiled, they were determined to maintain the holiness of the inner court.

This is of extreme importance to us. It is no great thing to point out the many ways in which the outer court has fallen, although it surprises me that more people do not see it. Even so, being able to articulate all that is wrong is of very little use if we cannot with equal conviction state what our response to it should be. After we see the problems with the outer court, there seems to be only two viable options: stay where we are and try to change it, or forsake it and go deeper. It seems that all of us, at one time or another, have tried to "change the system" but sooner or later we have met with frustration and aggravation. Immediately when we receive light from the Lord we want everyone else to walk according to that light, but it does not happen. So the only real choice is to go deeper.

The sons of Zadok decided that the outer court was not worth saving, and they sought to preserve the sanctity of the inner court. They did not try to change the outer court, they simply left it in favor of the inner court. It was either that or lose the whole Testimony.

Forced to make a choice, they decided to minister to the Lord.

Eventually both courts were restored. The sons of Zadok are a type of overcomer, standing in the inner court, ministering to the Lord on behalf of everyone else, thus preserving both courts – even though to the people in the outer court *it seems* as if the ones in the inner court are doing nothing. Indeed, *it seems* as if the ones in the inner court have disappeared altogether, and they are, perhaps, written off as having "gone astray," when the exact opposite is true.

"They Will Come Near to Me... and Stand Before Me... And Offer Unto Me..."

> "They shall come near to Me to minister unto Me, and they shall stand before Me to offer unto Me the fat and the blood, saith the Lord God" (Eze. 44:15b).

Ezekiel 44 illustrates for us what it means to be an overcomer. When the Ekklesia as a whole has failed to maintain the Testimony, God will raise up Overcomers from within the Ekklesia who will maintain the Testimony on behalf of the others who are unable or unwilling to maintain it. People will ask, "Do you think I am an Overcomer?" But what does it matter what I think? I know you are called to be an Overcomer. But look to yourself and you will know instantly if you are an Overcomer or not. Everyone called to be an Overcomer, but alas, everyone does not overcome. We do not overcome because we are Overcomers; we are Overcomers because we overcome. Read that sentence again very carefully: because being called as an Overcomer does not make you one, but living as an Overcomer definitely means you are one. There is nothing mystical about it. It bears repeating that the Overcomers are no better than the rest, they simply rise up and fulfill God's original intention for them, while the others do not.

If you are an Overcomer then the Testimony of Jesus is present in you. Now looking at things as a whole, while the Testimony may be present in some individuals, it is clear that the corporate Testimony is broken down today. God is not the author of confusion, but confusion abounds in our churches. God is not the author of discord and strife, but discord and strife abound in our churches. So there is not a clear Testimony – it is, for the most part, unclear at best, and contradictory at worst. The Ekklesia as a whole has not fulfilled God's intention for it. That is another way of saying that the Lord's Need is not being met. His Desire is not being fulfilled. His Will is not being done. It is not enough for us to examine the outer court and make some cosmetic changes. If we have failed in the ministry of the inner court then we have failed altogether, and *that* is where the root of our problem lies.

Many people have come forward to give us a "New Testament" style or pattern for meeting together. Different forms of church government are being tried. Meeting in cell groups or meeting in homes is being presented as an alternative. The house church has at last begun to call itself a "radical movement." Before long it may very well turn into a sort of unofficial denomination. We do not want to question or criticize the motives of those involved, and some of these things are well and good, but we want to point out that all of these things pertain to the outer court. Very little if any emphasis is placed on the inner court at all. With some exceptions, there is little ministry to the Lord, no more or less than there is in a "regular" church building. Whether you meet in a church building or in a living room or under a tree, what difference does it make if you are, spiritually and mentally, in the outer court the whole time? It is not a new method or a new system or a new movement that we need, but a new heart that draws near to God to meet His Need in the inner court.

From the ranks of the outer court the Lord is drawing people to minister to Him in the inner court. We are not saying the outer court has no use. Again, we should see the outer court as a means to an End, as the path one must take in order to access the inner court. That is *all* it is: a path. The problem is when we become stymied in the outer court and take up our residence there, when the ministry to the people becomes more important than the ministry to the Lord, or worse, when *that* becomes the End, and we never go deeper, and still worse, when we prevent *others* from going deeper. The fact remains that some are discovering a deeper purpose for themselves in God than what lies in the outer court, and are pressing inward. It is not so much a matter of disillusionment as it is a matter of dissatisfaction.

So in the context of this passage, what must happen in order for us to minister to the Lord? It involves two preparatory things: "draw near" and "stand before Me." We cannot offer anything or do anything until we first draw near to Him and stand before Him. I wonder: how much time have we spent just standing (or sitting or kneeling or lying) before the Lord, just to minister to Him? Is this the foundation for everything we do, or is it an occasional thing we experience, as we try to fit Him into our busy schedule? The Lord of the work is more important than the work of the Lord.

What does the fat and the blood typify? It represents the presentation of our bodies as living sacrifices (Rom. 12:1). This temple is unique in that the altar is the center of everything. This temple is a square, and in the middle of the square lies the altar, upon which those who minister to the Lord offer up the fat and the blood. Clearly, the altar represents the Cross, for to minister to the Lord in this way means a complete and thorough death to Self. You see, in the outer court you might be a "somebody," but in the inner court you are a "nobody," because in the inner court Christ has the preeminence as All in All. There is no room for your ego or your title or your position. You are shielded from the prying eyes of others, hidden from the praise and the criticism of men.

Another interesting feature is the clothing worn by the priests who minister to the Lord in the inner court. We notice two things: first, they must wear linen so as not to produce any sweat (vv.17,18). Sweat represents the works of the flesh. In the inner court one must learn to stand, not to strive. "Peace, be still" is the order of the day. What a contrast to the noisy activity of the outer court. To not do what the Lord has told us to do is sin, but to go ahead and do what we have not been commanded to do is sin as well. The second thing we notice (v.19) is that they must change their garments when they go out of the inner court, and they must put them on again when they return. They are not allowed to wear their linen into the outer court. Yes, there are times when the priests of the inner court must go into the outer court, and we will discuss that shortly. But the reason for the change of clothing is interesting: "they shall not sanctify the people with their garments."

In other words, those who minister to the Lord in the inner court are not allowed to impart anything of the inner court to those around them. Again, the God of the inner court will not come forth to meet us in the outer court, we must go to Him in the inner court and offer up the fat and the blood upon the altar by taking up our Cross every day. This simply means that each of us must learn to seek God for ourselves. I cannot carry your Cross, and you cannot carry mine. We cannot rely upon others to touch God for us, no matter how spiritual or holy they seem to be. For that reason, the ones coming forth from the inner court *according to outward appearance* seem no different than anyone else. There is no room for them to glory in themselves. If we are not careful we may disregard them as no different than anyone else, but if we look closely we will sometimes see them "changing clothes" as they pass from the outer court, into the inner court, and back again. This hiddenness is not only characteristic of those who know the Lord, it is absolutely essential. It will require a sensitive heart, a discerning eye, and a listening ear to recognize and learn from them.

They Will Teach What is Acceptable and Unacceptable

"And they shall teach My people the difference between the holy and profane, and cause them to discern between the unclean and the clean" (Eze. 44:23).

If I may paraphrase verse 23, I take this to mean, "Those who minister to the Lord in the inner court are best qualified to teach others concerning what does and does not satisfy the Lord and meet His Need." It may be that we have done quite a number of things that are pleasing to us or to one another, but they are not pleasing to the Lord in the slightest. Thus, it is profane, and it is unclean. It is a blemished sacrifice, and it is unacceptable.

Again, in Romans 12, we see the terms "holy and acceptable" used in conjunction with the sacrifice of ourselves to God. The converse of that would be "unholy and unacceptable." Some people think God will just accept whatever we do in His Name. But we know that the Lord accepted Abel and his offering, but rejected Cain and his offering (Gen. 4:4,5).

Our inability to perceive, know, or discern the difference between what is and what is not pleasing to God will open the door to all manner of spiritual and religious deception. Abel knew that the Lord wanted "the fat and the blood," a life for a life, but Cain offered up something produced by his own sweat (good works) without stopping to think if he was truly meeting the Lord's Need. In essence, Abel stood in the inner court while Cain stood in the outer court. Both offered sacrifices, but one was accepted while the other was not.

I wonder: out of all the "sacrifices of praise" offered on a Sunday morning, how many are accepted, and how many are rejected? Listen to me! If only we would draw near to God and stand before Him to minister to Him we would come into possession of a remarkable sense of discernment as to the Lord's Purpose, His Kingdom, His Will, His Desire, His Need. Only then can we offer ourselves as living sacrifices, holy and acceptable to Him. His pleasure will be our pleasure, and His displeasure will be our displeasure. If we do not know what the Lord wants, how can we pray? How can we teach others? How can we obey the Master if we do not know the Master's will? And how can we know the Master's will if we do not know the Master? Only those who minister to the Lord can know the Lord.

I mentioned earlier that there are times when the priest of the inner court comes forth into the outer court. Here we see that though their primary ministry is to the Lord, they will on occasion have a ministry to the people. What do they do? They teach others the difference between the holy and the profane, between the unclean and the clean. They will demonstrate the difference between what Abel offers up and what Cain offers up. When the priests come forth from the inner court they teach people how to minister to the Lord, how to meet the Lord's Need, how to offer up sacrifices that are holy and acceptable to Him.

The Hebrew word "teach" in this verse is interesting. Among other things, it means "to lay a foundation" or "to establish." The basis, the foundation of all ministry is to the Lord first. Learning how to meet the Lord's Need, and then doing it, is what it means to be a priest of the Lord; teaching others to do it is even more honorable. We are not saying there is no place for ministering to people, but we are saying that it is of secondary importance. If we make the outer court more important than the inner court, then we have failed. If we have met everyone's need it means nothing if the Lord's Need has not been met.

The altar, the Cross, is central to Ezekiel's temple, because to devote oneself to minister to the Lord will require a death-attitude to everything outside of the inner court. The praise and the criticism of man, the expectations of people, the demands of family and friends, the many needs and opportunities that present themselves to us, our own aspirations and ambitions about what *we* want to do or what *we* are gifted to do, our own ideas as to what is holy and unholy, acceptable and unacceptable: all of it must go. Our fruitfulness is not what we are to one another, but what we are to Him.

Summation

> "I am their inheritance: and you shall give them no possession in Israel; I am their possession" (Eze. 44:28b).

What does it mean to minister to the Lord as a prophetic priest of the inner court? It means...

- *Not my will, but Your Will.*
- *Not my Kingdom, but Your Kingdom.*
- *Not my glory, but Your Glory.*
- *Not my needs, but Your Need.*

It means that in times past we may have served the Lord with the expectation of a future reward, but now we serve the Lord with the realization that He is our Inheritance now. It means that in times past we may have viewed prayer as a way to achieve our own ends, but now we pray in order to ensure that the Lord's End is achieved. It means in times past we were obsessed with our needs and getting what we wanted, but now we are obsessed with God's Need, His Desire, and making sure He gets what He wants from us.

It means that in times past our greatest joy was to be seen doing something for God, serving in the outer court, busy with many things; but now, being dissatisfied with that and having discovered Him, our greatest joy is sitting before the Lord in the inner court, quiet and stilled as a child, that we may know Him. In a word, to minister to the Lord is to be content and satisfied, free of ambition, conscious of needing nothing, since He is All in All to us. We were created to love Him; we were created to be loved by Him.

Oh Lord, make us ministers and priests unto You first and foremost. Teach us to come into the inner court and meet You there. Teach us to seek first Your Kingdom and Your Righteousness, Your Desire, Your Heart, Your Need, Your Satisfaction, Your Glory. You are our Possession, our Inheritance, and our Reward. May we never be satisfied with anything less.

Chapter Seven

God's Prophetic Remnant

"But Daniel purposed in his heart that he would not defile himself..." (Dan. 1:8a).

I n our time the Lord is working with a Remnant and is raising up Overcomers to represent His interests in the earth, a people who are in this world but not of this world. In spite of a general failure of the Whole, the Overcomers, as a part of the Whole, are fulfilling God's original intent for the Ekklesia.

The idea of a Remnant is not without its historical examples. Let us define exactly what a Remnant is. Simply put, a Remnant is this: a person or persons who fulfill the Lord's Purpose for the Whole when the Whole either cannot or will not fulfill it. As an example, look at Noah. During a time when violence and sin filled the whole earth, here is one man who alone is righteous and pleasing to God. The Lord judges mankind with a flood, but does not make a full end. He spares Noah and his family and makes a new beginning with them.

Another good example is Elijah. He complained that since he was the only prophet left, he was better off dead, so he asked God to take his life. God replied, "I have reserved for Myself seven thousand people who have not bowed down to Baal or kissed him" (1 Ki. 19:18). What an awesome Lord! The entire nation belonged to the Lord. Technically speaking, they were His chosen people. But in fact, only seven thousand of them were truly faithful to the Lord's Thought and Purpose for them. They had not worshipped any idols. It is a comparatively small number, but certainly more than Elijah thought.

The Remnant Principle is found not only among the righteous. You remember that when Abraham made intercession for Sodom he was able to convince God to spare the entire city if ten righteous people could be found. Unfortunately for Sodom there was no Remnant, not even a little handful of people standing in agreement with God's Purpose, and so the city was destroyed. Remnants can make a difference between life and death, between salvation and destruction.

Anyone could have had the place in God that Noah had. God did not have a quota for the faithful in Israel that stopped at seven thousand people. The Remnant is not a closed group. I heard someone say this many years ago: "Anyone can, everyone won't, but somebody will." That is the gist of it, you see. There is a whole doctrine called Remnant Theology, but that is not what we have in mind here at all. Let us be clear: a Remnant is not an exclusive, elitist circle of super-spiritual saints. Not at all. The promises are made to the "whosoevers." Anyone can be a friend of God! Anyone can overcome! But we know that everyone will not. Why won't they? I wish I knew why, I wish I could explain it, but I cannot explain it, and I just know it is a fact that everyone will not go on with God. We know it from history, we know it from looking around us right now. Everyone is not going to press into God, everyone is not going to seek His Kingdom, everyone is not going to lay down their life and follow Jesus. Not that they *cannot*, but they *will not*. There is nothing set in stone that says you are destined to be an Overcomer, but these other people are not. No, everyone is destined for it, but how many will actually go after it? Anyone can, everyone won't (in fact, a large majority will not), but *somebody* will. That group of "somebodys" who will is the Remnant.

The Remnant surfaces again in the Book of Revelation, and they are called Overcomers. The Lord addresses seven Ekklesias, and makes a special invitation to "he that overcomes." Six of the seven had serious spiritual issues that needed immediate correction; Philadelphia, the one exception, was undergoing tremendous persecution. But if we read through these messages we see clearly that the Lord is calling for a Remnant to overcome. Then the individual identities of these seven Ekklesias seem to fade away from that point forward and from then on all we hear about is the Overcomers.

The Remnant in Israel

How does the Lord get the attention of His people? First, He sends us His Word. If we will not hear His Word, He sends us the prophets. If we will not hear the prophets, what then? Quite simply, the Lord will have to use our circumstances to get our attention. And in the case of Israel, when every other, shall we say, "diplomatic" solution had been struck down and rejected, the Lord said, "It is enough. I will have to make a new beginning. I will judge My people and accomplish My Purpose through a remnant, a small remainder of faithful ones. No, I will not make a full end, but I will cause all of them to pass through the fire of affliction."

The Lord had done this on a smaller scale many times before. When we read the Book of Judges we see the pattern. The people fall into idol worship and the Lord allows their enemies to overcome them. After a period of suffering they cry out to the Lord, He sends them a deliverer, and they are set free. Things go well for a time and then the vicious cycle repeats itself. Just look at the longsuffering of God! All of these things are meticulously recorded for us.

The Book of Daniel chronicles one of the lowest points in Jewish history. The nation of Israel had experienced a steady spiritual decline over several generations. The Lord had a significant controversy with His people. You know that Israel was to represent the One True God, the Creator of all things. As such, they were to be a people set apart from every other nation on the earth. All other nations worshipped idols; Israel was to be the example and the means through which the Lord would be able to reach all the idol-worshipping nations. Israel was the first monotheistic nation in the world – that is, they only worshipped One

God, whereas the other nations worshipped many gods. So the entire nation of Israel was to be a corporate remnant: a nation created to fulfill the Lord's Purpose for all the nations (the Whole) when the Whole either cannot or will not fulfill it. That was why Israel came into being.

Obviously the nation of Israel could not maintain the Testimony of the Lord if they worshipped idols just like every other nation on earth. They would lose their distinctiveness altogether. The heathen nations were supposed to be able to look at Israel, see the great blessing, wealth, peace, prosperity, and presence of God she enjoyed, and forsake their idols in favor of the Living God. In short, Israel was to be a living witness. Of course, we know that Israel failed. Instead of maintaining the Testimony, she sinned just like all the other nations, worshipping idols. Even a cursory reading of the Old Testament shows that this was at the heart of God's controversy with Israel. How could a set-apart people bear witness to One God when their lives contradicted the very truth they were supposed to have?

Time and time again the Lord would send prophets to warn them. There were bright periods of reform and purging of idols, but the general direction of the nation was downward. As time passed they grew even more wicked and reprobate than the heathen nations. This presented quite a "problem" for God, although of course that is not the best way to put it, but it is a good way to describe it. Here is a people who are to be a light to the nations, and instead, are actually doing damage to God's Testimony in the earth. They are no longer exclusive, or separated, or set-apart: they are through and through no different than any other nation. They are commonplace, ordinary, polluted, and compromised altogether.

So what can God do about it? May we say that the Lord was committed to Israel because, quite frankly, if Israel failed, then the Lord no longer had a clear Testimony in the earth. The message to the nations would be, "Israel's God is weak; He cannot even control His own people. Just look at them! They are no different than we are, so their God must be no different than our gods. The God of Israel is nothing to fear." Obviously such a situation as this would be intolerable. Unfortunately, everything hinged upon this backslidden, rebellious, disobedient people. The Lord could not just go to another nation and start over with them. There was too much invested in these people. A relationship had been entered into, and promises had been made – Abraham, Isaac, Jacob, Moses, Samuel, David, all of them had a stake in this. But more importantly, the whole world was looking to see how the "so-called" Living God (as they said) would deal with His idol-worshipping people. The very glory of God among the nations was in question. How could things have deteriorated to this point? It seems, naturally speaking, that everything is lost.

The Remnant in Babylon

Once all other means had been exhausted, the Lord decided to deliver Israel into the hands of a pagan, idol-worshipping nation – Babylon. The prophet Habakkuk argues with God that Babylon is more wicked than Israel, so how does that establish any kind of testimony for the Lord? How can God let His people be conquered by pagans? But the Lord knows what He is doing. It is almost as if the Lord is saying, "Since you have forsaken Me for idols, I will give you what you want: a manner of life altogether apart from Me and dominated with idols of every kind. I will send you away into a foreign land and you will finally have what you have wanted. Since you want to be like the other nations, since you want to live like heathens, I will give you the opportunity. But I will secure a Remnant, and I will bring them back to their own land, and from henceforth idol worship will never be a problem with Israel again." Behold the wisdom of God!

Remember when the Hebrews complained that they were tired of the manna and wanted meat? What did the Lord say? He said He would certainly give them meat, and they would eat it until it came out of their ears. They would have all they could stand and it would make them sick. In a similar way, the Lord determined to give them all the idols they wanted as a way to permanently cure them of lusting for idols.

So the Lord brought the armies of Babylon to Jerusalem. The Temple was looted and destroyed, the city was burned, and most of the people were killed.

The rest were carried away captive into Babylon. Everything, it seems, is lost. The Testimony is broken down, seemingly beyond the point of ever being recovered. God has "forsaken" His own people and allowed a heathen nation to conquer them. Not only that, but the spiritual center of the nation – the Temple – was gone, and with it the sacrifices, the worship, the priesthood, the Law, the prophets, everything.

But let us get beyond the historical perspective and take a look at things from a spiritual point of view. We must remember that everything points to *Christ*. From the beginning God is working to achieve a particular End, and that is the revealing of Christ and the establishment of a Kingdom. He took one man out of a nation of idol-worshippers – Abraham – and revealed Himself progressively to him. Thus monotheism was born, and from this one man God sought to secure for Himself a nation of His own as something separate and distinct from every other nation. We follow the line through Isaac, Jacob, Joseph, Moses, David, and the kings. It reaches its zenith in David's reign; that is, Israel most closely resembled what God intended under David. Solomon started out well, but then came that damnable idol worship again! Immediately the nation is divided into Northern and Southern kingdoms, and things go from bad to worse. Eventually the Northern kingdom (Israel) falls, and later the Southern Kingdom (Judah) falls.

From the spiritual perspective it seems that God has failed in His attempt to secure a people for Himself. Can we really appreciate the gravity of the situation?

Christ has not yet appeared, and Israel has failed. At this point, satan says, "At last! I knew it would not last. The very idea of a holy nation in the midst of all the other nations of the world! A separate and distinct people! Ha! I believe it is safe to say that we have won. Christ will not manifest Himself, because Israel is no more. We have the victory!" Why did satan hate Israel? Not because Israel was something, but because Israel was the door through which the Christ would come into the world. To destroy Israel before Christ can appear is to essentially kill Him in the womb (Rev. 12:4,5).

Of course, looking in retrospect, we know that the Lord is not going to just let the devil upset His Purpose. What is so amazing about the Lord is that man cannot upset His Purpose either! The Lord has already spoken through Isaiah that Christ would come. But Jeremiah says that the Lord will allow Israel to be held captive seventy years before restoring them to their land. The issue here is not just a matter of real estate. We must see that the issue with God is the bringing forth of His Son into the world, and the place of that bringing forth and revealing is in Bethlehem. The place of His sacrifice for our sins is in Jerusalem. This is already predetermined. So the land must be restored to Israel before Christ can be manifest.

It is at this point in the history of God's dealings with Israel that the Book of Daniel begins. We begin with the carrying away into Babylon of a Remnant of people. It is important to understand the philosophy of Babylon towards the nations it conquered. When we understand their approach we will better appreciate the analogy between Babylon of old and spiritual Babylon today. When you are conquered by Babylon, they begin to turn *you* into what *they* are.

The Medo-Persians, who followed after Babylon, took a different approach. They calculated that a happy people are a content people and are less likely to rebel, and so they allowed you to keep your religion and your customs more or less intact. That is why Cyrus permitted the Jews to return to their land and rebuild the Temple. But not so with the Babylonians. If they worship a certain idol, then you will be expected to worship it too. If they eat a certain way, then you will have to eat the way they do. Since they speak Aramaic, you will have to learn Aramaic. In other words, there is no room in Babylon for anything other than Babylon. You cannot retain your individuality, your own unique perception of things. You will be assimilated into their culture, or you will die.

Now we see at once the basis for a conflict here. A Jew cannot just "be" like every other nation and still be Jewish. Granted, most of Israel had lost their distinctiveness, otherwise they would not have been in this situation to begin with. But we know that if God is going to see His Purpose fulfilled then He is going to have to save for Himself a Remnant. This Remnant will be sorely tested, because where they are heading, it will not be easy for them to maintain any kind of a Testimony. The hope is that somehow, someway, they will remain faithful to the Lord in the midst of universal compromise, and they will successfully come through the seventy years of captivity, return to

Jerusalem, and allow God's Purpose to continue pressing forward towards the revealing of Christ.

All the hopes and dreams of heaven are bound up with this handful of exiles! So much is riding upon this group. Will they be faithful? Will they persevere? Or will they breakdown completely under the pressure of a foreign nation, a pagan society? To be sure, satan and all the spirits of antichrist are closely watching these developments. Israel as a whole may have been destroyed, but as long as these Jews remain there is the chance – albeit a slim chance – that God will be able to see His Plan through to completion. We must understand that all the forces of darkness are going to focus themselves against this Remnant in an attempt to shut up the Testimony once and for all. This, truly, is a momentous and critical period. More than Israel is at stake: the very fulfillment of God's Purpose and Plan for redemption, the actual coming of the Messiah to establish His Kingdom, hangs in the balance.

Now who would ever believe that with this much at stake the first battle to be fought will be over a thing so insignificant as what to eat? Who would ever guess that the very fate of mankind rested on something as simple as food. But I tell you that most of the people failed in this very first test, this very small test, and immediately disqualified themselves. I pray the Lord will open our eyes to see the principle here!

We have no way of knowing exactly how many were taken away into Babylon. We do know that of this group some younger men were selected for intense indoctrination into the lifestyle and customs of the

Babylonians. They were selected to undergo a rigorous program in which they would be educated in the arts, sciences, and religion of a pagan nation. They were to learn a new language and new customs. Even their names were changed, for each one was now named after an idol. Babylon is quickly swallowing them up into its system.

So from the beginning satan attempted to destroy this Remnant. We know that out of all these young men, only four of them raised any kind of objection to the changes that were demanded of them. Only four! Do we mean to say that out of all these young men, everything is resting on four? Yes, that is what we find out from the Scripture. The majority were probably thinking, "I have seen my people killed, my home destroyed, and the Temple burned. We have been brought to this land and we will never see our country again. God has forsaken us. We might as well get used to Babylon. We're lucky to still have our lives after all that has happened. Maybe if we cooperate we will have a better time of it."

These boys were appointed a daily provision of the king's meat and the king's wine as part of their indoctrination into the Babylonian lifestyle. Most of them quietly accepted the daily provision as part of the program. In fact, what a blessing it is to have food and drink at all! "After all," they may have thought, "Why should we worry about whether we eat meat or drink wine, or keep the Sabbath, or any other Jewish law for that matter? That way of life is dead and gone. We can't be Jews here. The Temple is gone, the priests are probably all dead, so it makes no difference." So they took the king's meat and the king's wine. This is only symbolic of their final capitulation to Babylon. That sealed it. From that point on they were pretty much lost to the Babylonian system. If they were Jews, it was in name only, because they had compromised themselves.

But there was one young man who would not quietly accept all that was being offered to him. He watched the others sitting at the table around him, and smelled the king's meat as it was served to each of them in turn, and listened to the gurgle of the king's wine as it splashed into their goblets. Then and there a decision was made: "But Daniel purposed in his heart that he would not defile himself with the portion of the king's meat, nor with the wine which he drank" (Dan. 1:8a).

Is Daniel merely jealous for the Law of Moses here, or is there a greater motivation? The point here is really not the meat or the drink, but the purposing in Daniel's heart not to defile himself. That there is one who would even make such a purpose is astounding, considering the circumstances. The easiest thing to do is to just go along with things, accept them as they are, and not make any trouble. But thank God for that decision! Daniel purposed in his heart – a flame was kindled, and the longer he thought about it, the hotter the fire burned. While the others were eating and drinking, Daniel motioned to his three friends, and whispered, "Eat mine if you will have it – but I will not sin against the Lord in this thing!" And the three brothers, Hananiah, Mishael, and Azariah, agreed that they would not eat the meat or drink the wine either.

Hallelujah! This is what the Lord is after – a small company of two or three, gathered together under a covenant that they will stand for the Testimony of the Lord, for something Heavenly, regardless of the cost! But why do you maintain your integrity, Daniel? Do you think you are better than everyone else? What do you hope to gain? What is the point?

Daniel and his friends represent the Overcomers. Daniel purposed in his heart that he would forever and always maintain a certain amount of hostility and resistance to the world system there in Babylon. Not a loud, demonstrative, attention-getting resistance, but a quiet, purposeful, principle-based way of living that would only allow him to go along with things up to a certain point, but then no further. Yes, he might be forced into the Kingdom of Babylon physically, but he refused to be forced into it spiritually! His God and his religion were not bound to a Temple in Jerusalem, to a priesthood or a system of worship. Daniel is saying, "It is true that the Temple is destroyed, Jerusalem is burned, and God has allowed us to be conquered. That does not change the fact that He is the Most High God, the Creator of Heaven and Earth. I am not changing my witness just because of my circumstances. I will maintain the Testimony of the Lord, even if it means death. I would rather die than defile myself and be disqualified from God's Kingdom. Someone, somewhere on this earth must represent the Kingdom of God, and though I may be *in* Babylon, I am not *of* Babylon!" That, in essence, was his reasoning.

The Remnant Today

What is the significance of these things, and what is the application to us today? Simply put, the time in which we live is no different from Old Testament Israel or the New Testament Ekklesias of the Book of Revelation. When we survey the landscape of Christendom we see one huge disappointment, an unbelievable immaturity, gross spiritual blindness and deception, and such a mixture and compromise with this world that there is virtually no distinction at all between the natural, the soulish, the fleshly, the carnal, and the spiritual. I will not spend a lot of time on that, because it is apparent to anyone with spiritual perception. As a whole, the Institutional Church has failed to bear the Testimony of Jesus, just as Israel failed to bear the Testimony of the Lord.

"Love not the world," the apostle John writes, "neither the things that are in the world. If any man love the world, the love of the Father is not in him. For all that is in the world, the lust of the flesh, and the lust of the eyes, and the pride of life, is not of the Father, but is of the world. And the world passes away, and the lust thereof: but he that does the will of God abides forever" (1 Jn. 2:15-17). This is clearly exemplified in Daniel.

Is that not the very foundation of our conflict today? Here we are, with a heavenly calling, a heavenly citizenship, a heavenly Jerusalem, a heavenly Temple, a heavenly Kingdom, but we are "exiled" for now in a world system that is trying every way it knows how to get us to defile ourselves through compromise. Clearly it is doing a good job. Just like those young Hebrew boys, we eat the world's meat, drink the world's wine, and generally act in a thousand other ways just like the world as part of the program and do not think twice about it. And we wonder why we cannot maintain a heavenly perspective! We wonder why we are not victorious! If we will purpose in our heart to set our affection on things above, not on things on the earth (Col. 3:2), then the Lord can do something for us. Until then, we are no different than the world, so why should the Lord do anything on our behalf? What kind of message would that send? Oh yes, you can eat the world's meat and drink the world's wine and carry on like everyone else and still have your religion and your God too? Not so!

In the end, Daniel and his three friends were found to be ten times wiser than the best that Babylon had to offer. When we align ourselves with God's Eternal Purpose then He will take us in and commit Himself to us in a powerful way. Once He has secured for Himself a Remnant then He will ensure that all of heaven backs them up, for they represent all that is meant by, "Your Name be revered, Your Kingdom be established, Your Will be accomplished *on Earth* as it is already accomplished in heaven."

Of course, such a people separated unto God for holy purposes will be marked by the enemy as well, those spirits of Antichrist that are opposed to God's Will and Purpose in Christ. We represent no threat to the enemy so long as we are engaged in our own trivial pursuits and little projects. He is not moved one bit by our religious works, meetings, or preaching, for most of this is done without any correlation to God's Eternal Purpose in Christ. We may bluster about in circles for years and never truly meet the enemy – we do not disturb him, so he does not disturb us. But as soon as we grasp something of the significance of God's Ultimate Will and begin moving towards a Heavenly Testimony in the earth then we represent a most serious danger to these principalities and powers.

The occasion of the conflict is the very revelation of Christ upon which the Ekklesia is built. The reality is that "the gates of Hell will not prevail against" this Ekklesia of the ones who have seen the Christ, the Son of the Living God, by the direct revelation of the Father; but this statement implies that the gates of Hell will certainly *try* to come against this Ekklesia that Jesus is building, which is itself a Remnant, a called-out people. Called out of what? Called out of Babylon; in the world, true, but not of the world. In Babylon, but standing for God's Kingdom, Power, and Glory in the midst of things completely hostile and contrary to that Testimony. It is not a question of geography, but Testimony regardless of geography. We will see this demonstrated time and time again as we progress through the Book of Daniel.

Chapter Eight

God's Plan for His Remnant

"[The Lord] reveals the deep and secret things: He knows what is in the darkness, and the light dwells with Him" (Dan. 2:22).

We are progressing through the Book of Daniel to identify the Remnant Principle. In the first chapter of Daniel we see that the Lord has reserved for Himself a remnant of four Jewish boys – Daniel, Hananiah, Mishael, and Azariah – to represent the Kingdom of God in the midst of Babylon. In the midst of universal compromise and failure, these four represent the Overcomers, those who maintain the Testimony on behalf of the Whole when the Whole either will not or cannot maintain that Testimony.

The spirit of Antichrist will always attempt to pollute what it cannot destroy, and destroy what it cannot pollute. We see this evidenced in the Scriptures time and time again. In the time of Daniel, the enemy has succeeded in getting Israel to pollute itself. Everything is compromised and the Testimony is broken down. From the perspective of darkness everything seems to be going in their favor – with the exception of Daniel and his three friends, who are determined to maintain the Testimony.

The conventional use of the word "testimony" means to make public confession, i.e., giving your testimony at church. In the Scriptural context, however, the Testimony of Jesus is much more than confession of Truth; it is the *demonstration* of Truth. I suppose we would be content to merely confess the Truth, but if we were never tested, it would never be demonstrated. For many, this is the case. Truth to them is a system of thought or a doctrine or a philosophy, but not an experience, not something that can actually be demonstrated.

The Book of Daniel holds within it the secret to being an Overcomer. Simply observe how in every case of conflict between the Remnant and the enemy that the Remnant is strengthened and the enemy is defeated. In every instance the very thing which meant to destroy the Remnant actually serves to reinforce it. I wish every believer would pay careful attention to this. How often we give up and quit, when if we had only remained steadfast, we would have been strengthened. Many times we are on the verge of a significant victory, breakthrough, or revelation but we give up when tested. The Book of Daniel will teach us to remain steadfast.

God's Plan

Now remember that in Daniel's time the powers of darkness are closing in upon the Jewish exiles. Daniel and his three friends stand alone against Babylon. They are the Remnant, the last link between God's Will and Kingdom in Heaven and His Will and Kingdom on Earth.

In a time of great spiritual darkness the Lord will remedy the situation by giving us a revelation of Himself. So in this case the Lord determines to reveal Himself in a powerful way, and the way He goes about it is interesting. He does not reveal Himself directly to Daniel as we might expect, but the initial revelation of Himself and His Kingdom comes by way of the pagan king Nebuchadnezzar. Is the Lord limited at all? We limit the Lord so much with our doubt and unbelief, saying God does not do this or cannot do that. Just you try to paint God into a corner and see what happens! The Lord says, "It is time to make Myself known and to reveal My Glory to the Remnant, to let them and the rest of the world know that in spite of all appearances, the Heavens do rule. And I will do it in such a way that My interests are secured and My Remnant is cared for all at once." What an awesome God!

So there are two sides to this plan of God. The giving of the dream is one aspect of the plan, but the giving of the interpretation is another aspect. The "difficulty" here is that there are many fortune-tellers and interpreters of dreams and "wise men" in Babylon. There are literally hundreds of potential interpreters there in that great milieu of astrologists and wizards. So the Lord goes right around that "difficulty" by giving the dream to Nebuchadnezzar and then taking it away again! This presents quite a frustration to Nebuchadnezzar, who knows he has dreamed something, but cannot remember what he dreamed. He has seen something, but cannot recall the vision. Nebuchadnezzar is no fool. He very cunningly demands that the wise men tell him both the dream *and* the interpretation, correctly surmising that if they cannot tell him what the dream is, how can he trust them to tell him the interpretation? Anyone can give an interpretation, but it would take a miracle to tell a man what he dreamed and tell him what it means, too.

The Chaldeans are taken aback. They respond that no one can tell the king what he wants to know, and no king in his right mind would ever ask such a thing. So Nebuchadnezzar, in his own warped sense of frustration and anger, orders the immediate destruction of all the wise men of Babylon. This sentence of death extends to Daniel and his three friends.

Now we went through all of that to get to this point: observe how the enemy would use the very revelation from God as the thing through which to destroy the Remnant. The adversary uses the very thing God intends to bless us with as a means to gain an advantage over us. Remember that it was God Who gave the dream, and it was God who then took the memory of the dream away. The enemy seizes the opportunity not only to shut up the revelation, but to destroy the people that he cannot otherwise defile. He cannot cause them to defile themselves, and he cannot touch them directly; but he can move Nebuchadnezzar to strike them.

We should consider how many instances there have been of the enemy getting the advantage over people through the very thing God intended for their good. A man is given great revelation, but becomes lifted up in pride and destroys himself with it. Or, a woman is blessed with a musical gift, but becomes enamored with the world and uses it for purposes other than the Kingdom. In the case of Daniel, the occasion of God's initial revelation was also the occasion of satan's attempt to destroy him. We repeat: if we want apostolic revelation then we must be willing to endure apostolic persecution.

The enemy *only* comes in response to revelation. Whenever the pure Seed is sown, the enemy comes *immediately*, either directly, or through difficult circumstances, or through deception and distraction in order to render that precious Seed useless (Mt. 13:19-22). We might imagine all sorts of "attacks" being carried out against us but the truth is that we are absolutely no threat to the devil whatsoever as long as we are fumbling about, doing our little religious duties, having our meetings, and talking about the Bible. He is not interested in this in the slightest, and is content to just let us spin our wheels indefinitely. Even when we go through the motions of "spiritual warfare" the enemy is unmoved. We are no threat at that stage. But let a little Light begin to come forth and then the enemy becomes interested because Light is the only thing that threatens the Darkness. The Darkness is not threatened by religion, spirituality, doctrine, loud music, preaching, crowds of Christians, spiritual warfare, prophetic conventions, or revivals. Darkness is only threatened by Light, and to the extent that we have Light, to that extent the Darkness loses its power over us. When we abide in perfect Light then Darkness has no power whatsoever. *And the light is nothing more or less than the revelation of Christ in His glory.* This truth is the underlying basis of Daniel's prayer to God: "[The Lord] reveals the deep and secret things: He knows what is in the darkness, and the light dwells with Him" (Dan. 2:22). Darkness and Light cannot co-exist. The Chinese have a proverb: do not curse the darkness, but light a candle.

So Daniel sought for more time to consider the king's request, and with the support of his three friends, made intercession to the Lord in order to know the dream and the interpretation. The Lord answered by giving Daniel the exact same dream that night, and wisdom to understand its meaning. We should see here that it is the nature of God to *reveal* Himself to all who seek Him. The purpose of all prophetic utterance and revelation is to make Him known (Rev. 19:10). Future events are revealed not for future events' sake, but to bring the preeminence and sovereignty of Christ to the forefront. So let us look at Nebuchadnezzar's dream, not to see history in it, but to see Christ in it.

The Rock Fills All Things

The dream is of a ferocious statue with a head of gold, a breast and arms of silver, a belly and thighs of brass, legs of iron, and toes of iron and clay. Then a rock smashed the statue's feet and broke the entire image to pieces. Then the rock grew until it became a great mountain that filled the whole earth.

The interpretation is that the statue represents a succession of worldly kingdoms. The head is Babylon, the chest and arms represent Medo-Persia, the belly and thighs represent Greece, and the legs and toes represent Rome. We are not going to develop that into detail, because that is not the purpose of the dream. The real significance of this dream is not that we know the identities of the world powers; the significant thing is this Rock! Oh, this glorious Rock upon which the Ekklesia is built, a Rock made without hands, which destroys the kingdoms of men and establishes a Kingdom that will never end! However terrible, ferocious, or strong these earthly kingdoms seem to be, they will be ground to powder before that Kingdom of God, and WE are kings and priests within this Kingdom!

"He must increase, but I must decrease" (Jn. 3:30). We see here the tremendous energy and power of God that is working to *increase* the Kingdom of His Dear Son and establish it "on earth, as it is in heaven." Along with the increase of the Son there is the *decrease* of all things opposed to the Son, the nations and kingdoms of this world, those things pertaining to antichrist.

May I say that the reality of that Rock is just as certain and sure as the reality of that horrible statue. Why are Bible teachers and students so enthralled with the statue, with tracing the histories of those kingdoms, but overlook the weight and significance of that Rock which grinds to powder everything that opposes it? The Rock, the Christ Who fills all things, is the point of the dream. Just as certainly as Babylon is the head, and Medo-Persia is the chest and arms, and Greece is the belly and thighs, and Rome is the legs and toes, so certainly is that Rock smashing it all to powder and is *increasing* until it fills the entire earth! Hallelujah! When we pray for the Kingdom to come and the Will to be done on earth as it is in heaven we are not praying vain, empty, useless words. We are calling for *Christ* to fill all things! And here we see the end from the beginning. The Lord reigns! His Kingdom is increasing, and His Christ will have the preeminence over all!

Take a good look at Daniel's initial revelation of the Kingdom. It is a simple statement, but it is the crux of the dream and interpretation:

> "In the days of these kings shall the God of heaven set up a Kingdom that will never be destroyed, and the Kingdom will not be left to other people, but it will break into pieces and consume all these kingdoms, and it will stand forever" (Dan. 2:44).

We note that:

- This Kingdom is established by the God of Heaven;

- This Kingdom cannot be overcome, destroyed, or defeated;

- This Kingdom will consume everything that opposes Christ; and

- This Kingdom will stand forever.

Hallelujah! I hope you are not looking to some future fulfillment of these things – in other words, I hope you are not looking *for* victory, but are looking *from* victory. When Jesus began His earthly ministry some two thousand years ago, He began to preach and to say, "Repent, for the Kingdom of Heaven is at hand" (Mt. 4:17). "At hand" means near, at the door, and has arrived. We certainly do look forward to a future consummation of all things, a future completion, but the foundation is already laid, and *in God's sight it is already accomplished*. He is Alpha as well as Omega. He is not Alpha in the beginning, and then Omega after everything is accomplished. He is both already. This is the basis of the Testimony of Jesus. Christ has already established His Kingdom, building the Ekklesia "upon this Rock" (Mt. 16:16-19), and through this Rock, is steadily filling all things.

Now which is larger in your sight? When you look upon the world today, do you see the horrible statue, or the Rock filling all things? "We do not yet see all things submitted to Him: but we see Jesus" (Heb. 2:8,9ff). In order to overcome, we must see that the Rock is larger than anything this world can produce. We must see a Christ and a Kingdom that is larger than this world, which is increasing, filling all things, consuming everything pertaining to antichrist, and standing forever. This vision, this seeing, is priceless. And this is what Overcomers demonstrate daily. If we have seen this, if we are convinced of its Truth, then we cannot help but order our lives accordingly. We will walk worthy of His calling. We will not allow ourselves to be infatuated with the world and the things of the world. How could we do that, knowing this Rock is consuming all things?

Jesus is building His Ekklesia upon this Rock, and the Rock is the revelation of Christ given by the Father. The Ekklesia is simply the synthesis of those to whom the Father has revealed the Son. This Revelation of Christ leads us to the Testimony of Jesus. When this Revelation becomes more real to us than anything we can see or hear or feel, then we are prepared to demonstrate the Truth that we proclaim, and the Testimony of Jesus is ours. *Through this Testimony* we overcome the dragon.

Overcomers Demonstrate the Truth

We cannot be called Overcomers unless there is something to overcome. In other words, if there is not something that rises up and challenges our Testimony then we are nothing more than hot air blustering about. As a matter of fact, the more sure our Testimony, the more severely we will be tested. Let us not imagine that the longer we walk with Jesus the less difficult our trials will become. By no means! As the Lord is revealed to us and we increase in the knowledge of Christ, our

Testimony is enhanced and enlarged, and with this enlargement comes tremendous conflict, spiritual pressure, and testing. How could it be otherwise? If we are not tested then all we have is a teaching. We cannot demonstrate Truth unless it is tested.

This matter of Testimony is something that cannot be received or apprehended in a sort of objective way. It has to be formed into you, it has to become a part of you until the Truth is not just something you talk about or teach, but is something you live. This is why I say that the *messenger* is the *message*. Hearing the messenger is more important than listening to the message he brings. The "lovely feet" of the messenger is what makes the message so wonderful (Isa. 52:7). We ought to be able to tell immediately if the message is a part of the messenger, or if it is just something obtained out of a book, or repeated from someone else. Do they just possess a message, or does the message possess them? Anyone can stand up and deliver a message, but it takes many years of God's dealings to work the message into the messenger so that the messenger *is* the message.

Before I knew the Lord I always had to pray, fast, study, and work very hard at preparing my sermons. It took many hours to put together a teaching. The teaching would turn out well, but the Life was not in it. Now when I go somewhere to speak I never have to prepare myself in advance. I do not need to find a quiet place to pray. I do not require a moment to be alone. I do not have to have a place to think and write out some notes. Why not? Because my whole life is preparation. I am the message. I do not bring it, I live it. I am presenting Christ, and I do not have to get ready in order to bring Him forth. The best thing for me to do is stay out of His way! If you have to "gird up your loins" and get yourself ready to say something then you are not living it. If you are living it then you cannot prepare for it. Either you are prepared or you are not prepared. But nothing you do in the last hour or so is going to make you any more prepared if you are not abiding in the Truth at all times. Abiding is essential.

So living out the Truth is more than just mentally comprehending it and reciting it. We overcome the dragon by the Blood of the Lamb, the word of our Testimony and by the laying down of our lives (Rev. 12:11). What is the Testimony? The Testimony is simply the Revelation of Christ as All in All being demonstrated in the lives of the Overcomers. There *must* be a demonstration, it must be existential, it must be living, and it must be incorporated into the very essence of who and what we are: and for that reason, there is a test. Whenever we apprehend something of the Lord, to the extent that we receive insight and perception into His Person, to that extent we will be, and we must be, tested in order to get the Revelation out into the open as Testimony; to take what we have seen and heard and make it known.

For example, let us say that the Lord gives you light to behold Him as Victory. By the grace of God your eyes are opened to see that the Lord Jesus does not give you the victory, but that He has given Himself to you as Victory. The difference is incalculable. You rejoice in the Truth that is revealed to you. "Thank God, the Lord Jesus is my Victory! I believe the Word of God. From henceforth I will not seek victory as a thing, for Christ is Victory!" Strangely enough, it is not long before something comes around to test the validity of your revelation. This is the common experience of all the saints. Simply maintain your ground, and the enemy will flee. Thus, Truth is demonstrated.

When the Lord first revealed Himself in me I thought that it would be smooth sailing from that day forward. Not so! I found that everything rose up before me as if to challenge what had been revealed. All of my circumstances gathered against me and seemed to be telling me that I was a fool and nothing I believed was true. Many "witnesses" came forth and gave very convincing proof that Christ was *not* my Victory, and that I must *do* something about it. Immediately I had to decide if I was going to believe what the opposition said or believe what God said. This was quite a temptation! Watchman Nee said that satan really only has one thing to tempt us with, and that is, to bestir the saints: to get them upset and cause them to rise up and *do* something instead of resting in the promises of God and the finished work of the Lord. Oh, I was sorely tested! But what it amounts to is believing the Lord or believing everything to the contrary. I determined to believe the Lord, and in time these circumstances completely dissolved before my eyes. It was a miracle! *The Truth of Christ's victory was demonstrated.* Thus, the Lord secured for Himself a Testimony, and I have no trouble confessing today that my victory is a Man, for Christ is Victory!

Victory Through Christ

We can say a thousand times that Christ is our Victory, but if in the heat of the moment we live like He is not our Victory, then the Truth has not been demonstrated and we do not have a Testimony. The problem is this: we pray *for* victory instead of praying *from* victory. We look *for* victory instead of looking *from* victory. How glorious it is to stand *from* victory and *see* the Truth demonstrated!

The Lord has enlarged me to see that Christ has spoiled principalities and powers, making a show of them openly and triumphing over them in the Cross (Col. 2:15). If I have truly seen this then I cannot be the same. How many Christians will nod their head and give their amen to this wonderful truth – but then go forth with a warfare mentality, trying to fight the devil as if there is something Christ left undone that they still have to perform? How does that demonstrate the preeminence of Christ? How does that maintain the Testimony of Jesus? It does not. We should give our amen to this, and then we should live like we believe it. This, to us, is no longer a Bible verse, but a statement of Truth, and we see it demonstrated constantly.

Or what about 1 Corinthians 15:57? The Scripture plainly says, "Thanks be to God Who gives us the victory through our Lord Jesus Christ." For most people that is just a verse, just one of the promises of the Bible. They do not see the Truth. They do not see Victory as something that is theirs already *through* Jesus. They do not see the word "gives" as meaning that there is nothing for them to do to merit or obtain this victory. But the Scripture is clear – God *gives* us the Victory *through* Jesus Christ. This takes all of the fight and struggle out of it. Victory is *given* to us! And it is not through anything I do or have done or can do, it is *through* Jesus!

Many Christians try to overcome by receiving a little of the Lord's power in order to help them get the victory. May we see before God that He does not give us power to overcome, but He gives us Christ as our Victory. He does not give us a few promises to confess in order to possess victory, but gives us the Victory through the Lord Jesus Christ.

If I am able to do a lot of spiritual things and apply them to my circumstances so that I overcome, who gets the glory? Who gets the credit? If I do the work, I will claim the credit – maybe not consciously, but unconsciously, I will believe that it was my fasting or praying or Scripture study or my great spirituality or something that gave "me" the victory. But if Victory is something God *gives* me *through* Christ then I have absolutely nothing to do but open up my arms and receive HIM! In this way, who gets the credit? Who does all the work? Christ gets the glory and the honor and the praise, and we are the recipients of so much grace, so much that is freely given us.

John writes, "For this purpose the Son of God was manifested, that He might destroy the works of the devil" (1 Jn. 3:8b). Since darkness gains its power solely upon the basis of deception, and not from any intrinsic power, any revealing or unveiling of Christ is hotly contested. To the extent that we see *Christ*, to that extent the enemy has lost power over us. It is just that simple. What a waste of time to "come against" everything and fight it head on. Such an approach will keep you occupied from morning until night, and from night until morning. No! The only way to destroy darkness is to bring in the Light, and all we need is the revelation of Christ. This revelation, this unveiling of the Son of God, is sufficient to defeat the enemy. When He is manifest then the devil's works are destroyed; hence, there is nothing for me to "come against" at all. The Rock merely consumes everything.

This is the reason why we have the Book of Revelation. In a time of great darkness, persecution, apostasy, and falling away, John is exiled to the Isle of Patmos. As the last of the Lord's twelve apostles, to be sure the present crisis was heavy on his mind. What is God's answer? A new spiritual warfare technique? A new formula for overcoming? A new promise to confess? The names of every territorial spirit? No, no, no, no! He simply pulls away the veil of the flesh, brings John into the Spirit, calls him up into heaven, and brings him into a deeper revelation and enlargement into the Person of Jesus Christ as *preeminent over all things. That* is the solution, not any kind of revelation into spiritual warfare, territorial spirits, and doctrines of demons. Everything pertaining to darkness is predicated upon a lie, and one of the greatest lies perpetuated is that you have to fight darkness by understanding the darkness. Nonsense! What futility! What frustration! How depressing! They say you have to "know your enemy." No, you have to *know your Lord*! Let us *behold the Son in His fullness*, and we will observe the darkness fleeing away before the brightness of that glory!

I have produced three verses from the Bible in order to demonstrate the preeminence of Christ over all things. With a little thought I could produce many more. We all know these *verses*, but do you know this *Man*? Do you only see Colossians 2:15, 1 Corinthians 15:57, and 1 John 3:8, or do you see Christ? Do you have three portions of Scripture, or do you have Christ? Do we have the Bible as a "thing" we can use as some kind of objective "sword," or do we have the Living Word demonstrating Himself through us? The difference between the one who overcomes and the one who is defeated hinges upon whether these truths are mentally assented to or spiritually apprehended. If we can quote them, or even teach them, in a disconnected, dispassionate, objective sort of way then we will never enter into the experience of it.

Daniel said, "The dream is certain, and the interpretation is sure." Daniel received the same light as Nebuchadnezzar, but Daniel ordered his life according to that light, while Nebuchadnezzar only satisfied his curiosity with it. Is this talk of victory, overcoming, and Christ filling all things just a teaching to you? A doctrine? A theory? An interesting Bible study? A history lesson? Or is this Kingdom and this Rock and this Victory a certain thing, a sure thing? May it be certain and sure in us! Amen! Even so, come Lord Jesus!

Chapter Nine

God's Ultimate Intention

"Upon whose bodies the fire had no power..." (Dan. 3:27ff).

T he Book of Daniel contains encouragement and wisdom for us who are being raised up as a Last Days Remnant of Overcomers. It records a succession of attacks against the Lord's Remnant and how they overcame these attacks and demonstrated the preeminence of Christ. We have already identified some principles here. Let us review them briefly.

First, we note that whenever the Whole fails to bear the Testimony, the Lord will raise up for Himself a Remnant – a comparatively small remainder of people – who will fulfill the Lord's original and full thought for the Whole. They are not doing anything other than fulfilling God's original intent. To us it sounds so grand and special; the very word "Overcomer" seems to imply that we are better than the others who are defeated, when in fact, overcoming is the normal Christian life. The entire Ekklesia is, indeed, a remnant of people called out of the nations in order to bear the Testimony of Jesus. That is *our* corporate calling, and to have anything less than that is abnormal. But in the Book of Revelation we see that there is yet a remnant within the

Remnant, a band of Overcomers called to demonstrate the preeminence of Christ in the midst of an Ekklesia that has failed in its corporate responsibility. So that is the situation we find ourselves in today.

Second, we find that whenever the Lord seeks to recover His Testimony in the earth by raising up a remnant, the enemy will come around to test the validity of that testimony and either try to spoil it through compromise, or destroy it altogether.

Third, we observe that the Lord's answer to a state of decline is to reveal Himself and His eternal purpose. Once the Lord has established for Himself a people that will represent His interests then He will move immediately to secure, protect, establish, and strengthen the Remnant. Here is what I want us to see. When we align ourselves with God's Thought, with God's Kingdom, and with God's Will in Christ, we are invincible. This is the secret to overcoming. It is not asking God to come down to where we are and bless our little ministry or work. Not at all. Instead, we leave our ground altogether and come onto the Lord's ground. We leave our earthly position and align ourselves with Heaven. We discern what the Lord's eternal Purpose is, and we set ourselves to cooperate with *that*. And when we are thus in conformity to *that* Purpose, all of Heaven is moved on our behalf. When our ministry or work is in harmony with that great movement of God, then we cannot help but overcome.

God's Ultimate Intention

We simply do not have enough respect for the tremendous energies of God that are moving in relation to the revelation of His Son. We cannot channel this for our own ends. That is like trying to capture lightning in a paper bag. And that is what we are doing when we go about things according to our own thought and mind and ask God to involve Himself with our projects. There is no end to the number of ministries, outreaches, and programs being initiated and carried out in the Name of Jesus. But of all these ministries, outreaches, and programs scarce few of them are actually aligned with God's universal Will; they do not have the Lord's End in mind. The work fills a need, but not God's Need; the work gives a sense of purpose, but there is no sense of God's ultimate Purpose. There seems to be little, if any, harmony with God's eternal Plan.

The "church service" does not provide a service to the Lord, but to us. It is not so much the service that I have a problem with as the sense of disconnectedness to God's ultimate Plan. From the perspective of Heaven I look down at all these church services and gatherings and meetings and what do I see? I see little hurricanes of activity, spinning around in a circle, disconnected from each other, and worse, having no correlation to God's Thought. Just an endless succession of services, gatherings and meetings that fulfill no purpose outside of themselves. A lot of wind and noise, but going nowhere.

What is the problem here? The problem is that we have lost that sense of Ultimacy. Most Christians do not understand the meaning of "preeminence," and even those who do, find it difficult to articulate it as God's Purpose for Christ, or even understand the ramifications of such a preeminence upon themselves, the Ekklesia, the world, and all Creation. That is not meant as a criticism, but as a statement of fact. Their vision penetrates no further than their own little world. The entire object of their faith is to make things more bearable for them here on earth. God is there to save them, heal them, and provide for them. Heaven is something to sing about and a place to look forward to, but it is not a present reality and the object of their affection here and now, or something to be demonstrated and brought to bear upon earth's "reality." Church exists to get them through from one meaningless week to the next. The ministry exists to keep them propped up and pumped up.

We are afflicted with a chronic smallness. Our God is too small, our Jesus is too small, our perception of Heaven is too small, our idea of church is too small, our concept of following Jesus is too small. Without a vision we are a small, petty, trifling people. May God give us the revelation of Christ! Oh God, give us that vision of Him! If we are illuminated to see Him then we cannot remain small any longer. He is God's Answer for smallness. This Testimony is a boundary-breaking thing, an overshadowing thing, an expansive and increasing thing: "Of the increase of His Government and peace *there will be no end*" (Isa. 9:7a). Not only will there be no end of His Kingdom, but there will be no end of *His increasing*! Oh God, we cannot fathom that! We cannot comprehend that! It cannot be contained. We cannot take it and fit it into our program. We have to find a way to fit into *it*, and not the other way around.

The Enemy's Intention

In the third chapter of Daniel we have the third assault upon the Remnant, and we are immediately confronted with the spirit of Antichrist. Right here in the plain of Dura, in the middle of Babylon, is a gold idol which is sixty cubits tall and six cubits wide. Well, here is that number six representing man, and here is an image set up by man, and a decree from man that all men should worship it, or die.

Oh yes, we thought that Nebuchadnezzar would have learned something from that dream and interpretation, did we not? But no, he is as wicked as ever, just as self-centered as ever. Truth to him was just something to fill his appetite for knowing what he did not know. He still does not know it. He will not be changed by it. The cost is too great. He is a poor, dumb pawn in the hands of darkness, blinded by his own pride and selfish ambition.

Where is Daniel during this crisis? We do not know. He is not mentioned in this account, so perhaps he was away on the king's business. What an opportune time for darkness to move in and attempt to overtake

Hananiah, Mishael, and Azariah. The enemy has despaired of its covert attempts to be rid of them, and now he brings everything out into the open and challenges them with what appears to be an insurmountable trial. If they bow down and worship the idol then the enemy wins; and if they refuse to bow down and worship then they will be thrown into the fiery furnace, and the enemy still wins. Either way, the enemy gets what he wants. There seems to be no way out of this one.

Now how would we respond to this situation? If Babylon represents the spiritual antichrist at work in the world system today then may I say that the 60 x 6 gold idol is still requiring you to bow down to it. It confronts you every day on this earth and is requiring that you pay it homage. There it is, plain as day, and the easiest thing in the world is to bow down to it – give in a little, compromise a little, let yourself go in this area, don't be so strict in this or that, and so on. All the while this beautiful music is playing, and it seems so right, so justifiable. Besides, everyone else is doing it! Even other "Christians" are doing it, so why not you?

The Temptation

What is *the* temptation? When we take the thousand and one little temptations and put them all together, to what end are they trying to bring us? Is there an overriding purpose for all these varied temptations we face? I believe there is, and I believe it can be summed up in this one passage of Scripture:

> "Little children, keep yourselves from idols" (1 Jn. 5:21).

This verse seems totally out of place in that first epistle of John, and appears to be an anti-climactic ending to such a beautiful letter, but it is actually a very appropriate ending. John is the apostle of Testimony, and he has summed up for us exactly what an Overcomer is. But let us quote this from the Amplified Bible for even greater insight:

> "Little children, keep yourselves from idols (false gods)–[from anything and everything that would occupy the place in your heart due to God, from any sort of substitute for Him that would take first place in your life]."

So what is he saying? On the one hand, you have God's Ultimate Purpose which says that Christ will have the preeminence in all things, beginning with each disciple individually, and with the Ekklesia corporately, and with all of Creation collectively. On the other hand, you have these false gods represented by anything and everything that would attempt to occupy the place in your heart due to God, and every sort of substitute for Him that would take the first place, the preeminent place, in your life. It is a direct challenge to the preeminence of Christ, the quintessence of antichrist, trying to gain the preeminence for itself so as to rob Christ of His position.

This, to John, bears directly upon the Testimony of Jesus. Just look at his words in his third epistle:

> "I wrote unto the Ekklesia: but Diotrephes, who loveth to have the preeminence among them, receiveth us not. Wherefore, if I come, I will remember his deeds which he doeth, prating against us with malicious words: and not content therewith, neither doth he himself receive the brethren, and forbiddeth them that would, and casteth them out of the Ekklesia" (3 Jn. 10).

What is the heart of the controversy here? Is John just jealous because Diotrephes does not recognize his apostleship? No, that is not the issue at all. John is jealous, but he is jealous for *the preeminence of Christ*, for that is the very essence of the Testimony, the whole reason for the Ekklesia to exist. And here is this man, Diotrephes, taking the preeminence for himself! This is untenable to John. He calls this evil, and says anyone taking the preeminence in this way has not seen God (verse 11). Are we prepared for such a confrontation? Can we handle such language? Pastor, how will you fare under that sort of spotlight? Prophet, will you pass the test? What about you, Apostle? And you, Deacon? And you, Elder? And you, Reverend? And you, Pope? And you, High Priest? And you, Televangelist? And you, Worship Leader?

I doubt that we are ready for a truly apostolic man. We give a lot of weight and attention to the "prophetic," and that is needed, but we need to look at an issue of equal importance: what exactly constitutes something as "apostolic?" An apostle is someone sent to set things in order, to establish things upon a foundation. It implies that there is either no order, or disorder; either no foundation, or a wrong foundation. And the "order" is *Christ first* and everything else beneath Him. The foundation is *Christ as All in all*. You need to get that. It is not bishops, elders, and overseers running around poking their noses into everyone's business, demanding submission to themselves – free spirits trying to get a following who will pay them tithes. These ones are just Diotrephes reincarnated, loving the first place, making a name for themselves. Nothing about them has changed in two thousand years. John says it is *antichrist*, it is *evil*, and these people *have not seen God*.

What makes John apostolic? First, he has seen and heard something. He has the Revelation of Christ. He has seen God's End. Second, he is apostolic because he burns with jealousy against anything which attempts to take the preeminence over Christ. To John, anything taking the preeminence for itself in the Ekklesia that Jesus is building is antichrist, and anything giving it the preeminence is idolatry. He has put his finger on Diotrephes, and says, "The whole problem with this man is he loves the preeminence. He has taken upon himself that which is due Christ, and Christ alone. For that reason, *if* I come, I will remember his deeds." Even as an apostle, he did not force himself into the situation and exercise some kind of human power.

That, in and of itself, would have just been an exchange of one kind of preeminence for another. John will wait until he is asked: but *if* he comes, he says, he will set it right; he will set it in order; he will secure the Testimony of Jesus in that assembly.

That is the sort of radical, uncompromising attitude he says we must exercise over our own hearts, for as the disciples go, so goes the Ekklesia. Just look at the gravity of his words! "Keep yourself from *anything* and *everything* that would occupy the place in your heart due to God, from *any sort* of substitute for Him that would take first place in your life." Fanatical, impossible directions! Do you really mean to say that there can be *nothing* that takes first place in my life but Christ? Is that what it comes down to?

Absolutely, that is precisely what is at stake, and that is precisely where the battle rages, and that is precisely why we are being tempted on a daily basis. Bound up in that is a lot of good things – spouse, children, friends. Bound up in that is a lot of religious things – church, ministry, work, calling, title, position. Bound up in that is a lot of reasonable things, a lot of moral things, a lot of innocent things. But the crux of the matter is: where does Christ fit in? All we have to do to be defeated is to put Him some place other than first. Either He is Lord *of* all, or He is not Lord *at* all.

The Testimony

If the Testimony of Jesus states that He will have the preeminence in all things, then how can we bear that Testimony if He does not have the preeminence in our own heart? If He has not first place *there*, how can we proclaim His preeminence elsewhere? We do not have to bow down to a literal idol, all we have to do is have some unsurrendered portion of our heart, some divided affection, a little love for this thing or that thing that tugs on us when Christ calls us to give it up, and we have already bowed down to antichrist. We have already taken the mark. Oh, it is a serious thing, a profound thing, and how we need to get before God and lay everything down! Otherwise, the Testimony is hindered. Do you see that?

There was no debate, no question among the Remnant as to whether or not they would bow down. "We are not careful to answer you in this matter." In other words, "We do not have to think about this at all. There is no anxiety on our part, not the slightest hesitation. We serve a Living God, and our God is able to deliver us out of the worst that you can deal to us, and He will deliver us out of your hand. We have aligned ourselves with Him that His Purpose may be seen in the earth, and you cannot stop that. But even if He does not deliver us, we will never serve your gods, and we will never bow down to your idol."

How were they able to maintain the Testimony? There was no hesitation in answering because they had already answered the question a million times before in countless temptations and testings all directed towards getting them to move just slightly to the left or to the right of the Narrow Path, but they would not budge. They overcame daily, and this, to them, was just another one of those daily things. A day in the life of an Overcomer. Here we are, just standing firm for God's Kingdom and God's Will. That is all. It makes no difference whether the idol is sixty cubits tall or six feet tall or whether it can be measured in terms of height and width at all. Whether it is meat, or wine, or women, or power, or position, or bowing down to this thing or that thing, outwardly or inwardly, we are submitted to a Kingdom that is filling all things, a Christ that is preeminent over all things, a Name that is above every name.

And you know the story, how that Testimony got them thrown into the fiery furnace. They fell down bound, into the midst of the furnace. I have seen television programs try to explain that the three men were in some cool corner of the furnace and that is how they survived. Yet the Scripture plainly says they fell into the middle of it. Right into the hottest part of the fire they were thrown, and it seemed for a moment that the darkness had overtaken them. "They did not bow, we expected that, but at last we are rid of them" they thought. But...

> "[Nebuchadnezzar] answered and said, Lo, I see FOUR men loose, walking about in the midst of the fire, and they have no hurt; and the form of the fourth is like the Son of God" (Dan. 3:25).

Go back to what I said earlier: when we align ourselves with God's Thought, with God's Kingdom, and with God's Will in Christ, we are invincible. I do not mean, of course, that we cannot die, or that we cannot be tempted or tested. Many have given their lives for the sake of the Testimony, and many more will. I mean "invincible" as something more profound than mere prolonging of earthly life, but *overcoming as He overcame.* Overcoming is not avoiding the evil, but persevering in spite of the evil. The Lord did not avoid death in order to overcome, but headed straight into Death, Hell, and the Grave, meeting it head-on, and coming out the other side in Resurrection. Death has no power over the one who has died and been raised to life; thus, we too must take up our cross, lay down our lives, and die that we may live.

Overcomers may not always avoid the fiery furnace altogether, but when cast into it they walk about in the midst of the fire. I am speaking figuratively, of course. The Bible talks about our fiery trials, and they are our portion. The fiery furnace is the means by which God may reduce us to Christ, and consume all that is of fleshly, natural origin. Like these three, we may go into the fire bound, but we come out unfettered. The dross is consumed, and the silver is refined.

Overcomers are those upon whose bodies the fire has no power (Dan. 3:27a). Put them in the fiery furnace and they are not consumed, only refined, only purified. It only makes them that much more conformed to the image of the Fourth Man, the Son of God, the Lord Christ. The fire has no power over them because the fire has no power over Him, and there He is in the midst. They do not seek the fiery furnace, but neither do they shrink from it when it comes. They do not ask for temptation and testing, but they are not afraid of it. They do not look for the devil behind every rock, but when they find him they demonstrate the preeminence of Christ over all things and call for his submission to Him. This is the Testimony of Jesus and the ministry of the Overcomers.

The Lord reveals Himself to us when we are at our end, when the fire burns the hottest. When we have reached the end of ourselves, then He intervenes. He is committed to us there in the fire, because we are committed to Him outside the fire. As we have stood for His Will and His Kingdom in a state of universal compromise, darkness, and deception, so He will stand with us in our state of temptation, testing, and trial. Towards what end? That the preeminence we have been proclaiming may be demonstrated. He will rise to the occasion and prove Himself faithful. "There is no other God that can deliver after this sort" (Dan. 3:29b).

Chapter Ten

The Rule of the Heavens

"The heavens do rule" (Dan. 4:26b).

I n the first three chapters of Daniel we find the spirit of Antichrist taking the offensive against the Remnant. In chapter one the point of conflict is their refusal to defile themselves with the king's meat and drink. In chapter two there is the threat to murder them along with all the wise men of Babylon. In chapter three they are thrown into the fiery furnace for their refusal to bow down and worship the idol. In each instance the enemy attacks the Remnant, and in each instance the Lord delivers the Remnant and preserves the Testimony.

In fact, the attack of the enemy is the basis upon which the Testimony is established. Just as there is no victory without a fight, no Crown without a Cross, so there is no Testimony without a devil. Our Testimony is not just "Hallelujah, I'm saved!" It is not a thing that is said, but it is a *life* that is lived. We overcome the Dragon by the word of this Testimony. This Testimony demonstrates the preeminence of Christ over sin, self, and satan: and it is a violent thing, a proactive thing, not a passive thing. The Lord's Testimony is actually strengthened when the enemy comes against it, for in the end we see that Christ is, indeed, preeminent. If we are really demonstrating this, then we should be getting stronger spiritually. That is not to say we will always feel good and always have a smile on our face while engaging the enemy. But regardless of our outward condition, our inward condition will be continually strengthened as we bear the Testimony of Jesus.

Heaven Governs Earth Through the Remnant

The fourth chapter of Daniel marks a turning point in our study. For here we find that this Testimony of Jesus is not always in a defensive posture. It is not always "under attack," but is just as much ON the attack as it is under attack. We have already seen that Christ, the Rock, intends to fill this earth, breaking and consuming all the kingdoms that stand in opposition to Him (cf. Dan. 2:44). Obviously this calls for destruction. "He must increase, but I must decrease" (Jn. 3:30). This is a very graphic, painful thing – to subdue all things to Christ, to put them down, to break them, to consume them, to decrease them. Just see how long and hard the Lord has to work in order to have the preeminence in YOU and in ME; to then imagine that same process being executed on a universal scale is nearly beyond comprehension. Yet we are assured that "He is able even to subdue all things unto Himself" (Php. 3:21b). What a mighty God we serve!

Exactly how the Lord goes about bringing all things into submission unto Himself is... how can we describe it? It is an art. It is a science. There is a process at work in this universe. Do you see it? It is a process through which the Lord is continually refining, purging, molding, chastening, disciplining, judging, and conforming all things. This process is working itself out on every level, from galaxies, to nations, to the innermost recesses of the souls of men, right down to the very last disciple and sinner. Throw yourself onto the Rock and be broken; or wait for it to fall on you and be ground into powder (cf. Lk. 20:18, Dan. 2:34,35). Either way, sooner or later, the Rock wins, for "He *must* increase, but I *must* decrease" (Jn. 3:30).

God has clearly relegated some of this work to the devil. He not only allowed, but practically invited, the devil to test Job. Job's end was better than his beginning, but what an awful time he had in between! It was the Spirit of God that led Jesus into the wilderness – not to conduct a private retreat or to experience a glorious revival, but to be tempted by the devil (cf. Mt. 4:1). Jesus prayed for Peter, but it is interesting that He did not prevent the devil from sifting Peter like wheat (cf. Lk. 22:31,32). And when Paul prayed three times for the Lord to take away the messenger of satan that was buffeting him, the Lord refused his prayer, but gave him Grace (cf. 2 Cor. 12:8,9).

What is His End? What is His Purpose? To "gather together in one *all things in Christ*" (Eph. 1:10ff). What a battle that is! What turmoil! Imagine the breaking that has to take place, the tearing down, the constant whittling away, the continual process of trimming, reducing, decreasing, crucifying. By the time you get to the End of the Narrow Way there is nothing left of you. But is that not God's Purpose in a nutshell? "Not I, but Christ" (Gal. 2:20ff). We still have a long way to go. But He *must* increase; therefore, we *must* decrease. And we can look here in Daniel 4 and see how the Lord goes about accomplishing this Purpose.

What Nebuchadnezzar had to learn is the same thing we all have to learn: the heavens do rule. Heaven governs Earth. To us who are still bound to the Earth it appears that we have a lot of authority, a lot of say-so, a lot to do with what happens here. But control is an illusion. We do not have control; indeed, we never had it to begin with. There is One Who rules Heaven and Earth. He is Sovereign.

The Decree of the Watchers Brings Heaven's Will Into Earth

To Nebuchadnezzar, of course, the Heavens are closed. He does not know the God of Heaven; he does not know that there is a Heaven. He is an Earth Dweller, and an Earth Ruler. He is the epitome of the natural man, the Adamic man. "Whom he would he slew; and whom he would he kept alive; and whom he would he set up; and whom he would he put down" (Dan. 5:19b). The natural man, the man of the flesh, just does whatever he pleases, whatever is right in his own eyes, whatever benefits *him*. He even dares to throw people into the fiery furnace if they dare to disagree with him.

May I say that all of us have something of Nebuchadnezzar living inside of us, this resident evil that only lives for Self. In the beginning Self flourishes like a mighty tree: strong and tall, with fair leaves and fruit – a dwelling place for the birds of the air and the beasts of the field. That was the dream Nebuchadnezzar had, a picture of himself. What a happy dream. What a delicious word of prophecy. He must have been quite pleased with the interpretation thus far. But as John the Baptist would say, "Even now, the axe is laid to the root of the trees. Therefore every tree which does not bear good fruit is cut down and thrown into the fire." (Mt. 3:10). Self is on a collision course with the Axe, and the bigger it is, the harder it will fall...

"Cut down the tree and destroy it" (Dan. 4:23ff).

It had been decided that this tree should be cut down and "his" (note the subtle use of personal pronouns here) branches cut off, and "his" leaves stripped. Yet a stump is to remain, tethered to the earth with a band of iron and brass, while "he" lives out in the fields, eating grass like an animal. And this shall be "his" fate until "seven times" pass over "him." Seven, of course, representing the number of completeness. It will be a very thorough work, designed to bring Nebuchadnezzar to the end of himself – and we cannot tell for sure if it will take seven days, seven months, or seven years.

Now that is quite a judgment. It leaves little to the imagination. But who made this decision? Who issued this decree? "This matter is by the decree of the watchers, and the demand by the word of the holy ones" (Dan. 4:17a). What is the decree of the watchers in verse 17 becomes the decree of the Most High in verse 24. Is it possible that the holy ones and the watchers made the decree because the Lord Himself had already decreed it? We believe so. We believe authoritative prayer is not expressing what we want, but expressing what the Lord wants. And if so, then the holy ones and the watchers are simply announcing what Heaven has already decided, and calling for it to come to pass. In essence, this represents the prayer ministry of the Ekklesia. This kind of prayer is for destruction. It is not for me to get what I want, but for the Lord to get what He wants. The selfish, the earthly, the egotistical, the carnal, and the fleshly cannot pray like this. But the watchers know how to pray.

Overcomers have power over the nations (cf. Rev. 2:26). Daniel himself was one of these holy ones, one of the watchers. Indeed, as Heaven's ambassador to Earth, he was the one who came down from heaven (spiritually speaking) to deliver this message to Nebuchadnezzar. For the first time in his life, Nebuchadnezzar was going to be personally confronted with a Power that is greater than himself, and a Kingdom which is greater than his own – a Heavenly Kingdom, which intends to come in by force and overrule his Earthly Kingdom. It is the "Rock that fills all things" (Dan. 2:34,35ff). Now, in this we see both the goodness and the severity of God. Love is fierce. Love will not be denied. Love never fails. And the Lord loved this pagan king so much that He was going to go to great lengths to break him. And not only for his sake, but to demonstrate His Preeminence to the world. "Whom the Lord loves, He chastens" (Heb. 12:6). What was the purpose? The purpose is the same, whether you are a sinner or a saint. The Lord intends to reduce you to Christ: more of Him, and less of you.

Earth's Submission to Heaven Not Optional

> "To the intent that the living may know that the Most High rules in the kingdom of men" (Dan. 4:23ff).

What is the purpose? That the living – Nebuchadnezzar and every other earth dweller – may know that the Most High God rules. He is Lord; He is Sovereign; He is Preeminent, though the Heavenly King is not always ruling openly. We still do not see all things submitted to Him (Heb. 2:8b). Yet, all things ARE under His feet (Eph. 1:22a). It is not always an outward demonstration of power, but it is definitely an inward, invisible, spiritual, eternal purpose at work beneath the surface, gathering "together in one *all things in Christ*, both which are in heaven, and which are on earth; even in Him" (Eph. 1:10b). And all of this is about to be demonstrated in the most unlikely of persons: heathen King Nebuchadnezzar.

The magnitude of this strikes Daniel with such force that he cannot speak, but merely stands there in astonishment for "one hour, and his thoughts troubled him" (Dan. 4:19a). At last he manages to give the interpretation to the King, and pleads with him to stop sinning and to begin showing mercy, in the hope that if he judges himself then he would not be judged of the Lord.

But even with this clear word from the Lord and this wise counsel, do you think Nebuchadnezzar listened? Do you think he really took it to heart? Nebuchadnezzar is like some people I know. They enjoy having prophets and wise men around. They say they want to know what God is doing and hear what God is saying. They like the prophetic word, and they like the prophet – from a distance, that is. They are all for confrontation, rebuke, and correction as long as they are not on the receiving end of it. As soon as it gets too close to home, then they are no longer interested in the prophet or in his prophecy. It would be too inconvenient for them to change their lives in order to live according to the truth of what they have been shown, so they ignore the truth, and continue on as before. Nebuchadnezzar had the same problem. So it comes as no surprise when we read that "all of this came upon the king Nebuchadnezzar, at the end of twelve months..." (Dan. 4:28,29a). He had probably forgotten all about what Daniel had said just a year earlier. But he would never forget what happened next.

> "The king spoke, and said, 'Behold, great Babylon, that I have built for the house of the kingdom by

the might of my power, and for the honor of my majesty!' While the word was in the king's mouth, there fell a voice from heaven, saying, 'O king Nebuchadnezzar, to you it is spoken; the kingdom is departed from you....'" (Dan. 4:30,31).

The Lord will allow Self to run its due course, just like the tree whose branches fill the earth and whose height reaches to the heavens. But a day of judgment is coming. Now, those who love Self will hate judgment; but those who hate Self will love judgment. If our heart is "not I, but Christ," then we will rejoice whenever we are decreased and Christ is increased. We will submit to the Lord's dealings with us. Our focus will not be on what Self loses, but on what Christ gains, for our loss is His gain. With less of me, there will be more of Him in my life, so why would I resist that? There should be less of me today than there was yesterday, and there should be more of Him now than there was before. If I will submit to Him today, then tomorrow there will be yet a little more of Him and a little less of me. Praise God! Spiritual growth is not stronger anointing, greater power, or increased knowledge. Spiritual growth is "He must increase, but I must decrease" (Jn. 3:30).

When Self is seen as the greatest hindrance to knowing Jesus then we will gladly let go of Self. We will not wait for judgment, but we will ask God to judge us right away. But first we have to see the flesh as an enemy. When we do, not only will we hate the flesh in ourselves, but we will hate the flesh in others. We will be repulsed by Self in us and will be sickened by the manifestations of Self in others. Paul says, "I know that in ME (that is, in my flesh) dwells no good thing" (Rom. 7:18a). Paul knows this. How did he know it? From trying and failing enough times to learn this lesson. At long last he is finally able to "rejoice in CHRIST JESUS and have no confidence in the flesh" (Php. 3:3b). Now, which will it be for us? Rejoice in Christ alone, or trust in our flesh? Our problem is that we still have confidence in our flesh. So we walk in the flesh. We make our flesh religious. We make our flesh "spiritual." But no matter how good, religious, or spiritual your flesh may be, "the flesh profits nothing" (Jn. 6:63ff). The question is not whether your flesh is good, religious, spiritual, or better than most people's flesh. The question is: is it flesh? If it is flesh then it profits nothing.

Every one of us – sinner and saint – are on a head-on collision with the Rock. Even now, the axe is at the root of the trees. I want us to see that the Voice from Heaven overrules whatever word is in our mouth. We may not be as bold as Nebuchadnezzar, leader of the pagans. Our pride may be a little more subtle than his. Yet the Heavenly Voice reveals us for who and what we are. God's Purpose for judgment is to subdue all things to CHRIST, to bring all things to the end of Self, so that CHRIST may fill all things (cf. Eph. 4:10).

Heaven Intends to Subdue Earth, Flesh and Self

> "The same hour was the thing fulfilled upon Nebuchadnezzar: and he was driven from men, and did eat grass like an ox, and his body was wet

with the dew of heaven, until his hair grew long
like the feathers of an eagle, and his nails grew long
like the claws of a bird" (Dan. 4:33).

It is apparent that Nebuchadnezzar went out of his
mind at this point. This moment of insanity was not the
result of a chemical imbalance, or a predisposition
towards depression. Remember that this judgment was
"by the decree of the watchers, and the demand by the
word of the holy ones" (Dan. 4:17a). The Remnant is
ruling! How long will this sentence be carried out on
him? "Until you know that the Most High rules in the
kingdom of men, and gives it to whomever He wills"
(Dan. 4:32b).

The sovereignty of God, the preeminence of the Lord
Jesus Christ, is what we have in mind here. Whenever
something untoward happens in the world someone
always has to remind us that "God is still in control."
Here is yet another reminder that this Rock is in
control (how many more reminders will we need?).
Nebuchadnezzar was kind of a cross between Hitler
and Saddam Hussein. My point is that humbling
someone like Nebuchadnezzar is a big thing, but not
too big for God. Upon this Rock some things will be
broken, and beneath this Rock some things will be
crushed; but whether you are broken to pieces or
crushed to powder, the Rock always wins in the end.
Get used to it! Embrace it! Surrender to it! Yield to it!
We cannot touch God and remain intact, for "our God
is a consuming fire" (Heb. 12:29). And this One Who is
the Consuming Fire is calling you by name, seeking you

out, and endeavoring to bring you closer to Him! If you want to go deeper into God, it is going to get hotter.

Pentecostals are fond of talking about the "fire" of the Holy Spirit in terms of power, charisma, and anointing. May I say that the fire of the Holy Spirit is but for one purpose, and that is refinement. This refining, purging, cleansing, and conforming to the image of Christ is the express reason the Lord Jesus Christ baptizes us "in the Holy Spirit and in fire" (Mt. 3:11b). The "Holy Spirit baptism" in Scripture is discussed in the context of judgment, refinement, and purification – not power, charisma, and anointing. Are you sure you really want to be filled with the Spirit? How many self-confessed "Holy Spirit baptized" people are as stubborn, proud, and unyielding as Nebuchadnezzar? They have not yet been through the fire, regardless of the experience they claim. The end result of a true Holy Spirit baptism is less of me and more of Christ.

> "And at the end of the days I Nebuchadnezzar lifted up my eyes to heaven, and my understanding returned to me, and I blessed the Most High, and I praised and honored Him that lives forever..." (Dan. 4:34a).

Once the fire has consumed every scintilla of Self; once the Rock has broken to pieces and crushed everything that resists it; once the things that can be shaken are shaken and removed; then the object of all this attention will be like the prodigal son who finally "came to himself" one day, and seeing the Truth, beat a hasty retreat back to His Father's house (cf. Lk. 15:17,18). The Lord, Who says, "I will draw all men unto Me" (Jn. 12:32ff); the Lord, Who "is not willing that any should perish, but that all should come to repentance" (2 Pet. 3:9ff); the Lord, Who "will have all men to be saved, and to come to the full-knowledge of Truth" (1 Tim. 2:4); the Lord, by Whom God will "reconcile all things unto Himself" (Col. 1:20ff); the Lord, before Whom "every knee will bow... and every tongue will confess" (Php. 2:10,11ff); this is the One Who holds Nebuchadnezzar now! Nebuchadnezzar, heathen ruler of the great world empire of Babylon, has been subdued. That is preeminence! *And it all happened by the decree of the Watchers* – the Remnant!

Before, Nebuchadnezzar could render lip service to the most High while retaining something of Self. But no more. It was a devastating blow to his pride to live like an animal, but at long last he "lifted up [his] eyes to heaven." As soon as he lifted up his eyes to heaven, his understanding returned. He "came to himself," and he immediately blessed God. That was the beginning of the end of judgment, for it had accomplished its intended purpose. Now he knew that "the heavens do rule," and he submitted to it, and God was satisfied. Glorious surrender! Knowing what we know now, would any dare say the cost was too great? Did God go too far? Was it too severe? Ask Nebuchadnezzar! He says,

> "I praised and honored Him that lives forever, whose dominion is an everlasting dominion, and

> His Kingdom is from generation to generation: all the inhabitants of the earth are reputed as nothing: and He does according to His will in the army of heaven, and among the inhabitants of the earth: and none can stay His hand, or say to Him, 'What are You doing?'" (Dan. 4:34b,35).

This is a genuine revelation of God's sovereignty, the likes of which we can only have when "seven times" have passed over us. There will be no forced idol worship or mass executions or "behold what I have built" coming out of Nebuchadnezzar anymore. The heavens do rule (they have always ruled), but now he knows it. And this Kingdom of Heaven is expanding and increasing – individually in each disciple, corporately in the Ekklesia, and collectively in all Creation – until *Christ* has the manifest preeminence in "all things" (cf. Col. 1:18b). What a mighty God we serve!

> "Now I Nebuchadnezzar praise and extol and honor the King of heaven, all His works are truth, and His ways judgment: and those that walk in pride He is able to abase" (Dan. 4:37).

I am sometimes asked how God will fulfill His Purpose of gathering "together in one all things in Christ" (Eph. 1:10ff). Friends, I cannot say how it will happen. Naturally speaking it is quite impossible. Theologically speaking it opens a can of worms. It goes beyond our comprehension, beyond my ability to articulate. But the issue is not whether we are smart enough to figure it out, but whether Jesus is big enough to pull it off. And I am convinced that even though I cannot say how it will happen, I do know that Christ is higher, deeper, and greater than we give Him credit for. With Him, all things are possible. And He is "working all things after the counsel of His own will" (Eph. 1:11b).

Now the Scriptures say that He is able to subdue all things to Himself (Php. 3:21b). It is not a question of "can" He, or "will" He. We do not have to wonder "if" it will happen. "And *when* all things shall be subdued unto Him, then shall the Son also Himself be subject unto Him that put all things under Him, that God may be All in All" (1 Cor. 15:28). "*When* all things shall be subdued unto Him..." See, it is only a matter of time. We see all of this coming to pass in the most unlikely of people, King Nebuchadnezzar. Nebuchadnezzar is Everyman. What does he say now? "Those that walk in pride He is able to abase." Herein lies the secret. God is *able*! And this same God is at work in all of us, and His Purpose is the same.

Earth's Resistance to Heaven is Futile

Daniel chapter four marks a turning point in the story of the Remnant. Heaven is on the offensive now, and the momentum is building. Something is breaking forth in the midst of Babylon, and the Remnant is central to all that is happening. As we progress into Daniel chapter five the conflict escalates. We meet King

Belshazzar, and see yet again that "the heavens do rule," but this time, the outcome is a bit different.

> "And you, his son, O Belshazzar, have not humbled your heart... and the God in Whose hand your breath is, and Whose are all your ways, you have not glorified..." (Dan. 5:22,23ff).

Some years later Daniel is once again brought before a king to give an interpretation. The occasion this time is the famous "handwriting on the wall," with the cryptic message that read:

Mene Mene Tekel Upharsin

We should note Daniel's boldness before Belshazzar as compared to his humility before Nebuchadnezzar. In bringing the word to Nebuchadnezzar he was "astonished" for one hour, and cried, "May it be to your enemies, and not you!" But before Belshazzar he minces no words. Belshazzar will die that very night. There is nothing left to salvage. And depending on Belshazzar's mood, Daniel could easily be executed for saying the things he said.

First, Daniel refuses the king's payment for providing the interpretation: "Let your gifts be to yourself, and give your rewards to another" (Dan. 5:17ff). What impertinence! Then he rehearses the history of Nebuchadnezzar, and recalls for the record how the God of Heaven humbled the king. Then he points the finger at Belshazzar and says, "And you have not humbled yourself, even though you knew all this!"

He accuses him of praising idols that cannot see, or hear, or know, and of ignoring the living God Who gives him the very breath he breathes. This is a strong word!

After he has successfully indicted Belshazzar, he is ready to provide the meaning of the words. The literal meaning is:

Numbered Numbered Weighed Divided

Now, even when we have the meaning of the words we still cannot say what the message is. Translating is one thing, but interpretation is another. We have Bibles full of words from the Hebrew, Greek, and Aramaic languages. We have many translations to choose from. Let us assume we can take a passage of Scripture and say that we have the correct translation. Very well, but the correct translation is not enough. The *interpretation* is from God. The ability to see beyond the words and actually read the message is of the Spirit. Knowing the Bible (as a thing) does not necessarily mean we know the Word (as a Person). Daniel knows the Word of the Lord because he knows the Lord of the Word.

> "God has numbered your kingdom, and finished it... you are weighed in the balances, and found lacking... your kingdom is divided and given to the Medes and the Persians..." (Dan. 5:25-28ff).

My point is this: do we have a "word from God," or do we have God Himself? Are we so into the next

‚rophetic "thing" that we have missed the Lord? Everyone sees the handwriting on the wall. A handful of people can translate it – but that does not make them prophetic. Only a Remnant can give the meaning. The Remnant, because it clearly sees God's Purpose, can accurately interpret all things through the filter of that Purpose. "It is the truth concerning Jesus that inspires all prophecy" (Rev. 19:10, Knox).

To understand the Lord's Will is to see that everything God has done, everything God is doing, and everything God will do; everything God has said, everything God is saying, and everything God will say; all of it relates to that eternal Purpose that He purposed in Christ Jesus. "Numbered Numbered Weighed Divided." What does it mean? It is a mystery until we have seen this Rock that Daniel talks about, which fills the earth. And that Rock is Christ. Here the message is to King Belshazzar. But I could walk up to any number of people and make the same pronouncement over them. Why? Because Christ is increasing, and they are decreasing. What is judgment to a sinner is salvation to a saint. If I am in Christ, then the end of "Me," the destruction of the Kingdom of Self, is cause for celebration! For then Christ will have the preeminence and I can say, "Not I, but Christ" (Gal. 2:20ff).

May I say that the handwriting is on the wall everywhere you look. What does it say? "He must increase, but I must decrease" (Jn. 3:30). That is just another way of saying, "Numbered Numbered Weighed Divided." I see the handwriting on the walls of our governments, our religious systems, our education systems, our financial institutions, and the nations of the world. They are all being decreased. But how am I able to see it so clearly? Because the same thing is happening inside of me! The same thing is happening inside of you! As He increases, everything else decreases. Do you understand this? If you truly understand this then you are the minority. You are part of the Remnant.

> "In that night was Belshazzar the king of the Chaldeans killed. And Darius the Median received the kingdom at the age of 62" (Dan. 5:30,31).

Escalating Tension Between Heaven and Earth

So the Heavens *do* rule. That is the point of the Book of Daniel. But how does Heaven exert itself upon Earth? How is God's Will performed? How is God's Kingdom established? Not directly, but through a Remnant. Not through angels, but through men and women, people who are "in the world," but are not "of the world." Remember our definition of the Remnant? A Remnant is a person or persons who fulfill the Lord's Purpose for the Whole when the Whole either cannot or will not fulfill it. They are the Overcomers.

So far we have traced the Remnant from Israel to Babylon. Nearly seventy years have passed since Israel went into exile and the Hebrew children refused the king's wine and meat. Daniel is in his eighties now, having spent most of his life on foreign soil, bearing a

Testimony that seems ridiculous: that the Heavens do rule. "If the Heavens rule," most Jews would have asked, "why did God allow us to be defeated? Why was the Temple and our nation destroyed? Why are we having to raise our children in this pagan society, far away from the Promised Land? And what about the Messiah? When will He arrive? Or is He not coming?"

How soon they forgot that the reason for their exile was idolatry and spiritual adultery. Yet, God has reserved for Himself a Remnant who will not be defiled. And through this Remnant He demonstrates His sovereignty. We have seen the Remnant delivered from an execution and a fiery furnace. And we have seen the Remnant exercise unearthly power over the very ones who had enslaved them, decreeing the humbling of Nebuchadnezzar and the elimination of Belshazzar. Tensions are rising. The Spirit of Antichrist is about to make another move. At the same time, Heaven is about to make a move. What happens when an immovable object meets an irresistible force?

We come now to the most significant crisis and spiritual conflict recorded in the Book of Daniel. Everything is leading up to this moment; eternity hinges on the outcome. Heaven and Earth are locked in a battle so fierce that once we understand the implications it will take our breath away. And everything is centered on the aged Daniel: sole survivor of the Remnant.

Chapter Eleven

The Prophetic Overcomer

I t would be helpful for us to review the principles we
have learned thus far. First, the Lord has a Purpose,
and that is for Christ to have the preeminence in all
things. In the language of Daniel, a Rock made without
hands will consume and break all other kingdoms into
pieces, filling the earth, and standing forever. Then a
Kingdom will be established that will never end (cf.
Dan. 2). Upon this Rock, Who is Christ, *Jesus* is
building His Ekklesia. That brings us right into the
present. This Purpose is as valid today as it was in 600
B.C.. Please do not relegate this teaching to history,
because if you do, then you miss the point and you miss
the blessing. The Book of Daniel will teach us how to
live according to God's Purpose *now*.

Second, whenever the Whole either cannot or will
not fulfill God's Purpose, the Lord will take a Remnant
out of the Whole in order to secure His Will on behalf
of the Whole. Of all the nations in the world, He chose
Israel to be the Remnant. Out of Israel, He chose a
handful of faithful ones to carry on the Testimony. Of
all the people carried to Babylon, Daniel and his three
friends were the only ones who did not defile
themselves. The Ekklesia is a Remnant compared to
the world, and the Overcomers are a Remnant

211

compared to the Ekklesia. "He gave some... till we *all*" (Eph. 4:11-13ff). The Lord uses *some* until He gains *all*. That is the Remnant Principle.

Third, whenever we touch something of God's Purpose, whenever we catch a vision of something of Heaven, whenever we see something pertaining to God's Kingdom and Will, we touch conflict. As soon as we grasp something of the significance of God's Ultimate Will and begin moving towards a Heavenly Testimony in the earth, then we become the subject of intense resistance from elements in this universe that are opposed to that Testimony. That resistance the Bible calls "Antichrist." It will always attempt to pollute or compromise the Testimony. If that does not work then it will attempt to destroy it. Remember that the Testimony is not simply stating, "Jesus is Lord." The Testimony is *demonstrating* the Lordship of Jesus with the way we live – by overcoming sin, Self, and satan. If we are not living in such a way as to demonstrate the preeminence of Christ over these three enemies then words are of little use. My Testimony is not something I *give*, but something I *live*.

Fourth (and we *must* get this), whenever anyone is aligned with God's Purpose and begins to pray for God's Kingdom and for God's Will, all of Heaven will be moved to support, strengthen, encourage, protect, supply, and fight on behalf of that yielded vessel. "The heavens do rule" (Dan. 4:26b). The Lord will immediately and decisively move to secure that Remnant. Daniel is a book of victory. It is a book of overcoming. Why? Because overcoming is the normal

Christian life of every saint who puts God's Kingdom and God's Will above his own kingdom and will. So take all four of these principles, put them together, and what you end up with is war in the heavenlies, unceasing conflict, and an almost unbearable tension in the spiritual realm.

This tension exists until God's Kingdom and God's Will are fully established. What *is* always resists what *will be*. Thus, the Lord Jesus does not tell us to merely wait passively for His return, but bids us to pray, "Your Kingdom come, Your Will be done: on Earth as it is in Heaven" (Mt. 6:10). Obviously, God's Kingdom is not yet fully established and God's Will is not yet perfectly fulfilled because life as we know it on Earth is not yet "as it is in Heaven." Far from it! Christ is preeminent, but He does not have the manifest preeminence; that is to say, Jesus is Lord, but "we do not yet *see* all things submitted to Him" (Heb. 2:8b). So Heaven and Earth are at odds until Earth gets into alignment with Heaven.

Three Characteristics of the Overcoming Remnant

When we *do* see all things submitted to Christ then God's Kingdom will have been established and God's Will, His Eternal Purpose, will have been accomplished. Then we can cease praying for the Kingdom to come and the Will to be done, for we do not need to keep praying for something to happen once it has already occurred. But until it happens we are called to stand in the gap and pray for its fulfillment. The deeper into spiritual conflict we go the more we begin to see that prayer, true prayer, is work; indeed, it eventually becomes our only work, our supreme work, for nothing happens until someone prays.

If God will do whatever He wishes, regardless of whether we pray or not, then we do not need to pray at all, and the Lord's instructions on praying for the Kingdom and the Will are superfluous. But the truth is that God waits for a Remnant to rise up and to pray in agreement with His Purpose before He does anything – He will do nothing apart from the Ekklesia. Apart from *Him*, we *can* do nothing; apart from *us*, He *will* do nothing. Here is my point: the Lord searches the whole Earth, and when He has found a person who sees that Purpose, and daily orders their life according to that Purpose, and (here is the key!) consistently rises up to pray for the fulfillment of that Purpose, then God will move Heaven and Earth on behalf of that person; for He has found, at last, some ground to build upon. That person is numbered with the Remnant because, I promise you, men and women like that are few and far between.

Daniel is such a person. Let us take the three characteristics I have just described and see how Daniel measures up.

First, Daniel has seen the Lord's Purpose. We will not take time to go through each prophetic chapter and study it in detail. But when you read through the visions and dreams recorded in the Book of Daniel you see one thing coming into view, and that is, the Eternal

Purpose of God. Everything Daniel sees or hears is interpreted through that Purpose. There is a thread that is woven through all of them, connecting them together. If we take the sum of them together, what do we see? We see the rise and the fall of earthly kingdoms, the coming of the Messiah, and the establishing of a heavenly kingdom that will never end. Now, this is stated in a number of different ways, but that is the message coming through every dream and vision recorded in this book. Christ will increase, and everything else will decrease (cf. Jn. 3:30).

Second, Daniel orders his life according to this Purpose. He is in the world, fulfilling his duty to such a degree of perfection that no fault can be found in him. He is not a starry-eyed mystic who neglects his earthly responsibilities. He is *in* the world, right in the midst of Babylon; but he is clearly not *of* the world. He has seen that Heaven rules, and the Most High is its Governor. He has seen the direction of the world, and he knows it is only downward. So he will be in the world, but he will not be of it. He will not eat the king's meat or drink the king's wine. He will not bow down to the idol. When no one else can give the interpretation, then he will give it, and he will not compromise the message. Kings can trust him with their business, and the Lord can trust him with His business.

I would like to take a moment to address this issue of "ordering your life" according to the Purpose. As Christians we have been preached to for so long that we often make the mistake of thinking that just because we know something to be true that we are then automatically ordering our lives according to that truth. But knowing something does not mean you are living by what you know. We must be on guard against smoothly assimilating messages and "words" with our brains. Receiving the Word into your brain will do nothing for you; the Word must be received into your heart. I do not want to hear congratulations and applause for an "enjoyable" message or a "thought provoking" article. I want to see us order our lives according to what we claim to agree with. As it is now, we are educated well beyond our level of obedience. We do not live a tenth of what we say we believe. Before we have put one message into practice we are anxiously anticipating the next. May God deliver us from partial obedience, which is only disguised disobedience.

Seeing something and living it are two different things. There is a difference between knowing the Path and walking the Path. Daniel is doing both, but he does not stop there. There is a third characteristic we need to see in him, and that is, Daniel rises up to pray for the fulfillment of God's Purpose. True prayer affords us the greatest opportunity for self-denial. When was the last time we offered up prayer, not for our agenda or plan, but for God's Kingdom to come and for God's Will to be done? When was the last time we came before the Lord, not to get our needs met, but to meet His Need? When was the last time we subjugated our own desires and wishes and gave ourselves wholly to praying for God's Purpose to be accomplished? When was the last time we separated ourselves from family, friends, and business and sought the Lord; not to receive a blessing *from* Him, but to be a blessing *to* Him?

We learn that Daniel was not only a man of heavy administrative responsibility and governmental authority, but he was preeminently a man of prayer: a man who withdrew from his earthly responsibilities in order to seek the face of the Lord – not once a day, not twice a day – but three times a day, offering up prayers, petitions, and thanksgivings before God. In addition to this, Daniel frequently ministered to the Lord with fasting.

Now, everyone wants power with God, but few want to deny themselves. They would rather just have someone pray for them or lay hands on them while they live any way they please. You know, there is no law that says a Christian must pray three times a day and serve God with fasting, like Daniel did. We are not led by rules and regulations, but by the Spirit. You can pray once a day, once a week, or not at all. You can eat three or four meals a day if you like, but I hope one day we will become hungrier for the Lord and thirstier for His Purpose than we are for our earthly food and drink. I hope one day we will become so consumed with heavenly things that earthly things begin to lose their grip on us. I pray we will at least have enough wisdom to understand that if we really want to know God we will have to pay a price for knowing. It will cost us something to obtain experiential truth, and it will cost us something to hold on to it after we obtain it.

Something should be driving us to pray. There should be some unction, some inner compulsion, to seek God, to seek Him early, and to seek Him often. If that is not our daily experience then something is wrong. Perhaps we have grown complacent, or comfortable, or cold. Whatever the reason, vision is the cure. If we have truly seen God's Purpose we cannot just go along as before. It will consume us. A person with a small vision will pray small prayers. Daniel is a man of huge vision, and so he prays large prayers.

I have said many times that everyone wants apostolic revelation, but no one wants apostolic persecution. We would like to have a gift like Daniel so we can interpret dreams, hear the voice of God, and receive prophetic insight into world events. Oh yes, we want the gift, but we do not want to pay the price. Is it any wonder that what is touted as "prophetic" today is simply "pathetic?" There is no depth of root in these people, no secret history of being dealt with by God, just an insane rush to bring forth yet another "word" that will satiate a greedy population's lust for something new and exciting (2 Tim. 4:3,4; 1 Tim. 1:5-7). New and exciting, maybe: but something the "prophet" has never actually walked in, and something which the people have no intention of walking in. They are ever learning, but never walking in the truth of what they have learned (cf. 2 Tim. 3:7).

Daniel has seen the Purpose; Daniel has ordered his life according to that Purpose; and Daniel is in the daily habit of praying for that Purpose to be fulfilled. Something bigger than himself is fueling his prayers. He is daily paying the price, living according to the Truth he claims to agree with, demonstrating the preeminence of Christ, showing that "the heavens do rule." So in him we see the Remnant Principle. Anyone who sees, lives, and prays according to that Purpose is marked out and set apart – marked out by the enemy, and set apart as the Lord's own possession.

Spiritual Warfare Beings with Prayer for God's Purpose

Let us turn now to the Scriptures and see this principle in action. In Daniel chapter 6 we see that in the first year of Darius the Mede, Daniel has been made the highest official in the former kingdom of Babylon, now a province of the Medo-Persian kingdom. The other officials are envious of Daniel and begin looking for something to accuse him of. But Daniel is faithful, and is without fault. They can find nothing to accuse him of insofar as his work is concerned.

So they realize that the only way to succeed against Daniel is to find something to accuse him of with regard to his devotion to the Lord. They devise a scheme and ask King Darius to sign a law which forbids anyone to pray or to request anything from anyone except the king, for thirty days. If the law is outrageous, the penalty is even more so: anyone who violates the order is to be thrown into a den of lions.

Obviously these officials had a special interest in trying to pass this strange decree, and it should have raised the king's suspicions. The text implies that they assembled hastily, and with great urgency. The king should have known better (later he would regret his decision), but he agreed with their request. And so, in the first year of Darius, for a period of one month, all prayers and petitions made to gods and men were outlawed under penalty of death. Now Daniel's enemies watched for the opportunity to catch him in his prayers, turn him in, and have him killed.

Since the Book of Daniel is not written in a strict chronological order, we may not realize the significance of the timing of this edict at first glance. But something else happened in the first year of Darius, and when we find out what happened, the reason for the attack of the enemy becomes plain.

We read in Daniel 9:

> "In the first year of [Darius]… I, Daniel, was studying the scriptures, counting over the number of years – as revealed by Yahweh to the prophet Jeremiah – that were to pass before the desolation of Jerusalem would come to an end, namely seventy years. I turned my face to the Lord God begging for time to pray and to plead, with fasting, sackcloth and ashes. I pleaded with Yahweh my God and made this confession…" (Dan. 9:1-4ff, New Jerusalem Bible).

The "first year of Darius" marks the end of Babylon and the beginning of a concentrated effort on the behalf of Daniel to fast and pray for the return of the Jews back to Jerusalem, for the rebuilding of the Temple, and for the coming of the Messiah, the Christ. Daniel was so urgent in this that he withdrew three times a day to pray. Whenever you decide to turn your face away from the earthly and towards the heavenly, towards the face of the Lord, you touch spiritual conflict. It is a battle to get into prayer, and a battle to stay in prayer.

So it is not coincidental that an edict outlawing prayer is suddenly proclaimed in the first year of Darius. As soon as Daniel rises up to pray for the fulfillment of God's Purpose, the enemy responds by threatening his life. The spirit of Antichrist is once again directly challenging the Remnant, threatening to destroy it, in an attempt to frustrate God's Purpose. Daniel has a decision to make...

> "Now when Daniel knew that the writing was signed, he went into his house, opened his windows towards Jerusalem, and kneeled down three times a day to pray and give thanks to God, just as he always did" (Dan. 6:10).

We might wonder why Daniel was so urgent about praying, fasting, pleading with God, and confessing the sins of his people. If God said seventy years had been appointed, and the time was complete, what more was there to pray about?

The answer is found in the prayer itself:

> "...And now, as it is written in the Law of Moses, this whole calamity has befallen us; even so, we have not appeased Yahweh our God by renouncing our crimes and learning Your truth... Yahweh our

God is just in all His dealings with us, and we have not listened to His voice..." (Dan. 9:13,14ff, New Jerusalem Bible).

At stake is the coming of the Messiah. Daniel correctly perceives that the seventy years had failed to bring correction to the Jews, and even though the allotted time was fulfilled, it might be delayed indefinitely as a result of the failure of the Whole. So Daniel, as a Remnant, rises up to pray for the fulfillment of God's Purpose, standing in the gap, and making intercession for the nation.

Daniel prayed toward Jerusalem. This is a symbolic act that is pregnant with meaning and there is an application for us today as well. We will come to that, but first, what was Daniel's reason for praying towards Jerusalem? No doubt he had in mind the prayer of Solomon:

"When they sin against You – for there is no one who does not sin – and You are angry with them and abandon them to the enemy, and their captors carry them off to a hostile country, be it far away or near, if they come to their senses in the country of their captors, saying, 'We have sinned, we have acted perversely and wickedly,' and turn back to You with all their heart and soul in the country of the enemies who have taken them captive, and pray to You, turning towards the country which You gave to their ancestors, towards the city which You have chosen and towards the Temple which I have built for Your name, listen to their prayer and their entreaty from the place where You reside in heaven..." (1 Ki. 8:46-49, Ibid.).

This is precisely what Daniel was doing on behalf of the entire nation. Chapter 6 of Daniel is concurrent with Chapter 9 of Daniel. Chapter 6 tells us that Daniel prayed three times a day towards Jerusalem while Chapter 9 tells us what was being said. While the enemy is plotting his death and trying to stop his prayers, Daniel says he is "confessing my own sins and the sins of my people Israel, and placing my plea before Yahweh my God for the holy mountain of my God..." (Dan. 9:20). The question before us now is: who will prevail? Which will come first: the answer, or the lion's den?

We have no way of knowing the exact sequence of events recorded in Daniel 6 and Daniel 9. We have some clues within the text. The enemies of Daniel quickly discovered that he had defied the edict and had continued with his prayers and supplications, so they immediately went to the king and demanded that he enforce the death penalty. We know that the king was upset with himself and tried "until the going down of the sun" to deliver Daniel before having him arrested and thrown into the lion's den (cf. Dan. 6:14). We also know that the angel Gabriel arrived to personally deliver the answer to Daniel's prayer "at the time of the evening sacrifice," which was sunset (cf. Dan. 9:21; Ex. 29:39).

It is quite possible that the events of Daniel 6 and Daniel 9 all occurred within the space of a few hours. I have found through personal experience that the lion's den usually comes about the same time as the revelation. The burden to pray comes with the edict forbidding prayer; Daniel labors for God's purpose while Daniel's enemies labor for his death; the answer comes along with a death sentence. This is not unusual, but quite common.

What is my point? Apostolic revelation and apostolic persecution go hand-in-hand. We cannot have one without the other. Revelation does not come to us apart from our circumstance, our environment, our struggle, and our wrestling. Many want the revelation, but they do not want the lion's den. They want the angels, but not the enemies. Yet the depth of the revelation is measured by the depth of the suffering, and if our sufferings are light, then our revelation is shallow.

The thing revealed to Daniel is nothing short of miraculous – not only that Christ is indeed coming, but the exact timing of his appearance:

> "Seventy weeks are determined... know therefore and understand, that from the going forth of the commandment to restore and to build Jerusalem unto the Messiah the Prince shall be seven weeks and threescore and two weeks..." (Dan. 9:24,25ff).

It is commonly understood that the "weeks" mentioned here are weeks of years. There is some dispute over the exact time, but most scholars calculate the sixty-nine weeks (483 years) to either the birth of Christ or the beginning of His public ministry. The point being that Daniel received a specific answer to his intercessory prayer and prophetic confirmation of the fulfillment of the very Purpose he has been praying into existence. Now he could face the lion's den with calm assurance that God would perform His promise.

The Remnant Stands for Heaven's Agenda

It is important for us to realize that Daniel is not praying from any sense of sentimentality for his own people. His concern, and the motivation for his prayers, is not for the sake of his nation, but for Christ's sake, for the Kingdom's sake. We are not suggesting that Daniel did not pray for and love the Jews, but we are suggesting that his primary motivation was to see God's Purpose fulfilled, of which the Jews were (and are) a part. Daniel was not a Jew who prayed for fellow Jews, but was a citizen of Heaven who prayed for God's Purpose to be fulfilled "on Earth as it is in Heaven."

We must pray as heavenly citizens of a heavenly kingdom, not as earthly citizens of an earthly nation. Most of the time Heaven's interests are at odds with what the nations want. If that is the case, we must side with Heaven, not with our own country. If we pray according to what the evening news says, or according to our inclination as citizens of South Africa, or Israel, or Australia, or Germany, or the United States, then we have failed our heavenly mandate, and God's Kingdom suffers loss. We may be praying for blessing and protection when the Lord is calling for decreasing and judgment (or vice-versa). *If we cannot separate ourselves from patriotism and nationalism then we cannot have power with God in prayer for His Kingdom.* Daniel was zealous for God's glory, not Israel's glory.

Here is what I want us to see. If we come to the Lord on the basis of being a Jew, or a Gentile; a Protestant, or a Catholic; a Fundamentalist or a Charismatic; an American, a Nigerian, an Israeli, an Arab, a Filipino, a Chinese, or an Argentinean; a rich person or a poor person; a professional clergy or a layperson; a male or a female; a red, yellow, black, or white person; then we are approaching the Lord solely on an earthly, human basis. We have to leave all our earthly ground and come onto the ground of *Christ*, and that is a heavenly thing. It goes beyond where we are.

Our history, our heritage, our lineage, our culture, the earthly things that we identify with, the things that make us who we think we are – all of it ends at the Cross of Christ. He is the Alpha: all things have their beginning in Him. He is the Omega: all things have their ending in Him. So my identity is not found in the fact that I am white, male, Charismatic, or American. "White power" and "black pride" and "rugged American individualism" is flesh: that is earthly, it is of the earth. It is death. We ought to avoid it like cancer. What is a Messianic Jew? What is a Charismatic Christian? What is a Fundamentalist? What is a Calvinist? What is a Baptist? What is a Methodist? What is a Catholic? What is a Religious Conservative? I tell you, there is nothing like that in Christ – these are all human contrivances. There are only two kinds of people in the universe. Either you are in Him, or you are not in Him. Everything else is just clutter.

I am not saying that you should shirk your responsibilities. Remember, Daniel was faithful in all his duties, and no fault was found in him. Yet he was able to separate what he *did* from who he *was*. His identity was not based on his position or his calling, but on his standing in Heaven. That is all that matters. I am asking you: are you willing to stop being an American? Are you willing to stop being a black woman? Are you willing to stop being a Charismatic? Are you willing to stop being a Methodist? What I mean is, *are you willing to be reduced to Christ and "just" be an anonymous follower of Jesus, a nondescript branch among many other branches who are abiding in the Vine, and leave your own identity behind?*

If you are unwilling to leave your ground and come onto the ground of Christ where everyone is equal, then you will never see anything from Heaven's perspective. Everything will be filtered through that earthly identity. But if you lose your life here, then you will find your true Life, and that Life is from Above, not Below. That is the secret to power with God. Earthly challenges (like a lion's den, for instance) cannot be overcome with Earthly thinking, Earthly attitudes, or Earthly prejudices. It takes someone from Above to subdue something from Below. It takes something Heavenly to confront something Earthly and prevail over it.

> "So Daniel was taken up out of the den, and no manner of hurt was found upon him, because he believed in his God" (Dan. 6:23b).

Daniel prevailed over Earth because he was of Heaven. Daniel prevailed over Darkness because he was of the Light. Daniel prevailed over Death because he had Life. Daniel was delivered from the lion's den, and lived to continue his ministry of prayer. After such an ordeal we might expect him to go ahead and retire, to quietly settle down, and relax a little bit. Certainly he has earned a vacation. But shortly thereafter we find him battling in the spirit for twenty-one days while he waited for yet another answer to be delivered from Heaven. Can there be any doubt as to the outcome? Daniel does not stop. This is what it means to overcome. You can never coast, you can never let down your guard, and you can never just let things slide for a day or two. Overcoming is not a once in awhile thing, it is an all-the-time thing. Settle that within yourself right now.

It bears repeating: the Lord searches the whole Earth, and when He has found a person who sees His Purpose, and daily orders their life according to that Purpose, and consistently rises up to pray for the fulfillment of that Purpose, then God will move Heaven and Earth on behalf of that person. If you are reading this I pray the Lord is speaking to you, calling you by name, saying, "You are the one I want!" I challenge you to lose your agenda and be devoted to Heaven's Agenda from this day forward, and every day, for the rest of your life. The Remnant Principle says that if you will seek first the Kingdom of God – that is, if you will put His Need, His Will, His Purpose ahead of your own needs, wants, desires, and plans – then He will not only perform His Will and establish His Kingdom, but He will protect, defend, and fight on your behalf. That is the only way to overcome.

The Lord in Search of Overcomers to Form His Remnant

Every Christian, every believer, every disciple can be that person. All of us are called to be Overcomers. It is for the "whosoevers." The Lord is seeking you as much as you are seeking Him. The Lord is calling out for Overcomers, those who have the Revelation of Christ and who bear the Testimony of Jesus; those who demonstrate the preeminence of Christ over all things. That is your purpose as a Christian – in fact, it has always been God's purpose for saving you and leaving you on the earth, whether you have realized it or not. You are *not* on the earth to be constantly disappointed, discouraged, and defeated. You are on the earth to demonstrate the preeminence of Christ; to show the world that "the heavens do rule." Daniel is living the normal Christian life. A defeated Christian is a contradiction: it is not your destiny. Rise up and live according to the truth: that Victory is a Man, and He lives inside of you, and the One Who lives within you is greater than whatever comes against you.

The Lord walks in the midst of spiritual Babylon, calling out for Overcomers, looking for those with a spirit like Daniel, who will pray daily for His Purpose to be fulfilled. We, like Daniel, pray daily for the Kingdom to come and for God's Will to be done. But our vision is higher and wider than Daniel's vision: "The Jerusalem which is from above is free, whose children we are" (Gal. 4:26). For Daniel, Jerusalem represented an earthly Temple and a holy mountain. Our Jerusalem is from above, and we are the Temple of the Holy Spirit (cf. 1 Cor. 6:19). We do not pray towards an earthly Jerusalem, but towards a heavenly Jerusalem, the New Jerusalem, which is coming down from God as a bride prepared for her husband (cf. Rev. 21:2).

We are not zealous for the establishment of any earthly nation, but for a heavenly nation of "kings and priests" (cf. Rev. 5:10). We are not praying for the building of a physical temple, but a spiritual temple, a house of living stones, of which Jesus Christ is the Cornerstone (cf. 1 Pet. 2:4-9). We are not looking for the appearance of an earthly Messiah, but a Heavenly Messiah, Who is building His Ekklesia upon the foundation of Himself, against which the gates of hell cannot prevail (cf. Mt. 16:18).

Though we are physically on the earth, we are not of the earth. This is not our home, for we are from above. Though in the world, we are not of it. We will not eat its meat or drink its wine, and we will not bow down to its idols. Though we live in the shadow of Babylon, we are not afraid of its fiery furnace or its den of lions, for our God is able to deliver us.

The heavens do rule. We affirm it boldly and confidently, regardless of appearances to the contrary. The Kingdom, the Power, and the Glory belong to God – not man, not the devil, not the nations of this world. The Most High rules in the kingdoms of men, and

Christ is increasing and filling all things. Have you seen this in the Book of Daniel? If you have, then embrace it, submit to it, cooperate with it, be in harmony with it, order your life around it, demonstrate it to the world around you, and pray for its fulfillment. Get aligned with something and Someone higher and greater than yourself. For when you see His Purpose, and order your life according to that Purpose, and consistently pray for the fulfillment of that Purpose, then His Purpose cannot be stopped; His Will cannot be frustrated; His Kingdom cannot be defeated. Heaven singles you out and Hell trembles with fear. You just became undefeatable! You just joined the Remnant.

Chapter Twelve

The Prophetic Savant

sa-vant' (n.): 1. a mentally defective person who exhibits exceptional skill or brilliance in some limited field; 2. a person who is highly knowledgeable about one subject but knows little about anything else.

"...the prophet is a fool, the spiritual man is mad..." (Hos. 9:7).

"What then is genius? Could it be that a genius is a man haunted by the speaking Voice [of God], laboring and striving like one possessed to achieve ends which he only vaguely understands?" – A.W. Tozer

(Note: the use of the male pronoun in this writing is for convenience only. We mean no partiality to our brothers, and no disrespect to our sisters.)

The prophetic savant is a person afflicted with a heavenly autism, making him nearly incapable of normal relations with those around him. Accused of being aloof, cold, and distant, he is apt to hide himself from people, withdrawing into a world of his own. He never seems to be all "there." Even if he forces himself to come down to Earth for a moment, those around him may have the sense that there is an unspoken dialogue going on somewhere inside of him, a secret communion carried on beneath the surface that never allows him to be fully "in the moment."

How do we explain this? As a prophetic savant he sees, hears, and relates to the world differently than the rest of the population. They have not seen what he has seen; they have not heard what he has heard. And so he finds very little camaraderie, very little sympathy or understanding, no one with whom he can open his heart and share his soul, because he no longer speaks the same language, and they no longer speak his. Of course, he may have surface-level exchanges with anyone: he is approachable, not haughty, or high-minded. He may even be personable and likeable. Yet there is something so other-worldly in his demeanor that he is more often frightening than friendly, in spite of his best efforts. He is a spiritual autistic, and no matter how hard you try to know him, he is generally unknowable, and to a certain degree, he resists all attempts to know him.

If a prophet is anything, he is extra-terrestrial – above the Earth. He walks the Earth with others, but he is not of the Earth. He is from beyond; he is from above. If we trace his history we will find that he may or may not have had a normal childhood. He may or may not have come through extraordinary experiences. But at some point in his life, either as a child, or as a young adult, or as an old man, something from another realm broke through the thin membrane between Heaven and Earth and took hold of him. It may have been a burning bush, or a Voice crying out to him from beyond the veil, or a Heavenly Vision which brought him briefly into contact with something and Someone that he could not completely fathom.

However it happened, for one moment at least, the clouds parted and the veil was rent, and he saw something that is unseeable; he heard something that is unhearable; Heaven itself was opened up to him, and he saw into another world. The thing he saw and heard now burdens him like a mantle that has been draped over his shoulders. He feels its weight, for it is with him day and night, whether he is eating or drinking, working or resting. It is the impression that everything around him is a lie, and what he has seen and heard is the Truth, and this Truth is not static, but it is living, growing, and increasing within him from the day it comes to him in the form of a seed.

For a long time he struggles to find words and vocabulary to express the inexpressible. He cannot explain why he feels the need to try and express it, but for some inexplicable reason something drives him to open his mouth, or take up his pen, and make it known. Whatever it is, it will not permit him to savor it or keep it to himself, and it seems intent on coming to the surface and interrupting the normal course of his life. This process can be frustrating and painful, so much so that he may give up several times, content to simply walk in what he has seen and heard and leave it at that.

But try as he might, he cannot run away from what he has seen and heard, and he cannot deny the compulsion to bring it forth. On the one hand he cries out for a "normal" life, while on the other hand he knows he cannot deny what has been revealed to him. When he does achieve some modest success in articulating something of Heaven he is pleased for a time, but soon grows impatient with it, and eventually is dissatisfied with it altogether, because it cannot do justice to what he has seen and heard. And so the process begins again, the continual search for words to more perfectly express what he is trying to communicate (and a subtle fear in the back of his mind that he may never be able to adequately express it), which leads him to invent words that may have never before existed, or to look for Spirit-inspired words in some unknown tongue that can be translated into something others can understand.

The prophets of old correctly called it the "burden of the Lord," for it is like a woman who must live the rest of her life being in perpetual labor, delivering the same child over and over again. What relief there is only comes in discharging the burden, but that is not to say it ever really leaves: it merely allows the prophet time to catch his breath until the next contraction doubles him over again. The burden is with him the rest of his life, and he never fully discharges it.

Even when he tries to be disobedient to the Heavenly Vision and flees from the presence of the Lord he is pursued and hunted down like some kind of a wild animal who has gotten loose, knowing it is only a matter of time before he is captured again. The Voice never leaves him, the Vision never lets him go. When he refuses to speak then the fire which is already kindled only burns hotter, until he ends up doing what he has resisted doing all along, just to relieve himself of the unbearable tension and inward pressure. He cannot extinguish or quench the fire no matter what he does, he can only be obedient and find temporary relief, until the next word comes, and then off he goes. He may beg God to send someone else, and may protest his inability to speak, or to write. But he is already ruined for anything else, and even when he denies the Lord Who called him and returns to his former occupation, it is all dull and lifeless, and he meets with nothing but frustration and failure. There is no way to escape it. He knows he is called to something Higher, even when he is clinging with everything he has to something Lower.

Like a wild horse, he resists the dealings of the Lord and must be broken before he will obey. Eventually he learns not to resist the Lord, but to cooperate with Him. He becomes pliable and bendable in order to survive. His very life now is bound up with what he has seen and heard. He cannot be disobedient to the Heavenly Vision, and if it means he dies, then he dies. If it means a renunciation of everything he once believed, then he renounces it – reluctantly at first, then cheerfully. If it means suffering the loss of all things, then he lets them go.

Over time the one who has seen and heard becomes the very essence of what he has seen and heard. The Man becomes the Message. He bears the Testimony in himself, and becomes one with it. He needs no preparation to speak; indeed, preparation does nothing to help the message he brings, and it often gets in the way. His whole life is the preparation, and since he is the Message, it is with him constantly. He can no more separate himself from the Message than he can separate his head from his body. If there is an "On/Off" switch then it was long ago turned on and then disabled so that it can never be turned off again. After many seasons of God's dealings he finally perceives that this is what the Lord has sought for all along, not just to *give* him a Message, but to *make* him a Message; to gain for Himself a Messenger and capture him completely, emgraving the Message into his very being.

And so he goes about his daily business, constantly haunted by that Voice, torn between the menial task at hand that calls for his physical and mental exertion, and the Higher Calling that seeks his undivided attention. He knows he should do all things, great and small, as "unto the Lord." But he also knows that Heaven and Earth are locked in mortal combat over him while he stands there in the middle, torn between the two, desiring to depart the Earth altogether and be with Christ, but knowing that it is more profitable for his brethren if he remains. Heaven calls him to rise up, but Earth tells him to keep his feet firmly planted. His heart is constantly breaking and longing to go, to ascend, to rise up, to stop seeing through a dark glass, and see face to face, without the distraction of the natural, the fleshly, the temporal, because he knows the Earth is not his home. Yet he struggles with the fact that Earth is where he must live and work. This accounts for why he may sometimes seem difficult to be around.

As a savant he possesses insight and skill that others do not possess. But it is a gift, not anything of himself, nothing of which he could boast of. If you were to ask him if he considers this to be a blessing, he would probably say it is more like a curse, because it sets him apart from others even when he tries his best to be hidden and to blend in. He cannot read the Scriptures as others do, for after only a few verses the Heavens are opened up to him again and he is lost in its depths. A single passage may keep him occupied for months as Heaven unfolds it to him, and he cannot tear himself away from it.

His preaching is affected, because he cannot decide in advance what he will say, and even when he would like to bring forth something new and exciting, he usually ends up saying the same thing, like, "Repent!" He often does not say what he wants to say, and does not say it in the way he would like to say it. If he wants to be serious, he finds himself laughing. And when he wishes to be friendly, he finds himself screaming at the top of his voice to a startled congregation of people, who wonder how this fellow was ever allowed access to their inner sanctum in the first place. When he leaves a place he almost never sees the result of his labor, and only eternity can reveal the true significance of what was said. For now, it is all hidden, and he has to live with the fact that his fruitfulness will never be measured in terms that human beings, including himself, can see and appreciate.

He cannot go through the motions of religion like most mortals. It is a dead, shallow thing to him because it cannot compare to the reality of what he has already experienced. He finds it difficult to listen to another person preach when he knows they have not yet ascended to the heights nor plumbed the depths that he has already navigated. And when he tries to lead them into these heights and depths himself he is often misunderstood or rejected altogether. So either he attends the meeting and suffers in silence, or stays home and suffers in solitude; but either way, he suffers.

His seeing is affected by a sort of "spiritual dyslexia." While others view things from a one or two dimensional viewpoint, he sees them through several dimensions at once – forward, backward, reverse, upside-down, right-side up: life and death, light and dark, Spirit and flesh, Heavenly and Earthly – which often puts him at odds with his more pragmatic and doctrinally-correct brethren. He is so at one with what he has seen that he speaks of it as having already happened, because he has, in essence, already experienced it and lived it. It is the Prophetic Tense, which calls those things that be not as though they were. In his world, the world of the Spirit, they exist already. We call it "prediction" because we cannot yet see it with our natural eyes, but he simply stands outside of Time and views Past and Future as one unbroken and continuous Present.

His hearing is affected so that he is increasingly sensitive to his surroundings, even though it seems as if he is not paying attention. He is listening, but he is listening inwardly. He no longer trusts his natural ears, because the Heavenly Voice and the inner witness are more reliable. Thus, he is able to hear God speaking, while the rest of the crowd says, "It thundered!" or "It was an angel!" He is also able to hear when God is not speaking, and does not get carried away with the multitudes who claim to speak, see, and hear things from God when they have not heard or seen anything from Heaven. He cannot bear to listen to them.

His concentration is affected in such a way as to make him appear obstinate and unyielding to others. The truth is that he is actually quite flexible and pliable before the Lord, but before man he is as solid and impenetrable as a rock. No amount of persuasion or argument from man will move him – but the slightest touch from the Lord will bring him to his knees. Having discovered the One Thing that is needed, he will tenaciously and ruthlessly shun the "many things" that crowd in to seek his attention, for he sees everything else as a distraction. Indeed, he is quite willing to sacrifice the good in favor of the holy. And when the Lord has him focused on a particular thing he is as a beam of light fastened upon a singular point until everything melts before it.

Even his praying is affected, for he can no longer pray as he wills and for what he wants. He seemingly has no will of his own. Instead the Heavenly Voice bids him to pray with a Heavenly perspective, and all too often the Heavenly perspective is at odds with the Earthly perspective. So when his brothers and sisters pray for blessing and increase, he finds himself praying for destruction and decrease; and when they are resisting and praying against something, he finds himself asking God to perform the very thing the rest of the world is against.

To the rest of the world, the autistic savant is a bit of a retarded genius, an unfortunate mixture of idiocy and brilliance, caught up in a world of its own. The prophetic savant bears a similar stigma. But if you engage him at all, you soon discover that he sees all of this as absolutely normal; the way it is supposed to be. He no longer wishes for a normal life, because the life he has now IS normal: he has lost his own life in exchange for a new life. He lives in the Heavenlies while he walks on the Earth. He does not think of himself as special, as anything other than a regular person, but often wonders aloud why others cannot see what he has seen when it is all so self-evident and plain. To him, maybe; but the rest of us are blinded by the Light he exudes without knowing it.

Chapter Thirteen

The Testimony of Jesus

"Having made known to us the mystery of His will, according to His good pleasure which He purposed in Himself, that in the dispensation of the fullness of the times He might gather together in one all things in Christ, both which are in heaven and which are on earth—in Him. In Him also we have obtained an inheritance, being predestined according to the purpose of Him who works all things according to the counsel of His will" (Eph. 1:9-11).

From this portion of Scripture we gather three facts that have been revealed concerning the Eternal Purpose of God. First, God does have a Purpose – a Will, an Intention, a Reason, a Motive, a Desire; something He wishes to accomplish. Second, this Purpose is centered around Christ. God wants to consolidate everything that is presently scattered, broken, and far removed from Him and restore everything to be in harmony with Himself through His Son – that is, "to gather together in one all things in Christ." Third, we see that God "works all things" according to this Will and Purpose; that is to say, everything God has done, is doing, and will do is connected with this Purpose of gathering everything together in Christ, merging heaven and earth into a Christ-centered universe. This is the idea behind the high priestly, prophetic prayer that Jesus taught His disciples: "Your Kingdom come, Your Will be done, on earth as it is in heaven" (Mt. 6:10).

The ultimate intention is "that in all things, Christ should have the preeminence" (Col. 1:14). The Ekklesia is (ideally) the one body of people on earth in whom Christ *already* has preeminence, in whom the Kingdom has *already* come, in whom the Will of God is *already* done; compared to the rest of the world that does *not* give Christ the preeminence, does *not* acknowledge His Kingdom, and does *not* do His will.

So there is quite a discrepancy between what God wants and what actually exists, but the Eternal Purpose states that Christ must have the preeminence *in all things*; this would include not just those in the Ekklesia, but all creation. This is prophetically expressed in many Scriptures, among them: "The earth will be filled with the knowledge of the glory of the Lord, as the waters cover the sea" (Hab. 2:14). These, and similar passages, express God's intention for Christ to have the manifest preeminence over all things – not just in theory, but in fact.

God's heart has always been for all people: "All the ends of the world shall remember and turn to the Lord, and all the families of the nations shall worship before You. For the kingdom is the Lord's, And He rules over the nations" (Ps. 22:7,8).

The Prophetic Testimony

Remember that the prophetic calling requires both *receiving revelation* and *declaring testimony*. So with the revelation of God's Eternal Purpose concerning Christ, there is a corresponding testimony that is declared. Scripture refers to this as *The Testimony of Jesus*.

As we have previously discussed, the very essence of the prophetic word revolves around the Testimony of Jesus (Rev. 19:10). The grand finale of Scripture records a great battle between the Overcomers and the Spirit of Antichrist concerning the Testimony of Jesus:

> "And the dragon was enraged with the woman, and he went to make war with the rest of her offspring, who keep the commandments of God and have the testimony of Jesus Christ" (Rev. 12:17).

What is the Testimony of Jesus? Why does the prophetic word revolve around this Testimony? Why does this Testimony attract so much rage, spiritual conflict and opposition? And what does it mean *to have* or *to bear* this Testimony?

To answer these questions, we must consider the circumstances around which this Testimony came to be, and the man God used to teach us its significance: the apostle John.

John: The Apostle of Testimony

If we look in the New Testament we see a natural order and progression of things. Matthew, Mark, Luke, and John discuss the earthly ministry of Jesus Christ. From here we move on to the Acts of the apostles, where we find the birth of the Ekklesia and the continuation of the Good News in the early saints. Then we move on through the letters to the Romans, Corinthians, Galatians, Ephesians, Philippians, Colossians, Thessalonians, Timothy, Titus, Philemon, Hebrews, James, and Peter. The majority of these letters were written to address particular problems or issues as they arose among the early believers, but they lay a foundation for us of things pertaining to Christ, the Ekklesia, and sound doctrine.

If we are careful and studious we will notice a shift beginning with 2 Peter. 2 Peter, the letters of John, and the letter of Jude were written much later, after the Ekklesia had been inundated with false brethren, false teachers, false prophets, false apostles, and false doctrines. Peter wrote his second letter after his first letter was rejected. John sums every false and heretical thing up into this one spirit he calls "Antichrist." Even Jude expresses a desire to write about the common salvation, but is then prompted to write instead concerning false prophets. This represents a fundamental shift from *general doctrine* to *prophetic admonition and warning*.

The books of the New Testament are not arranged in strict chronological order. Nevertheless, they are arranged in a particular order. First, that which concerns the earthly ministry of Christ; second, the record of the birth and acts of the early Ekklesia; third, the teachings and doctrines of the Ekklesia; and fourth, the warnings against false prophets and teachers, who by now have gained some ground.

If we stopped at this point, with Jude, we might conclude that things are being left undone. There is much that goes unanswered. So the last book in the New Testament is the Book of Revelation. This book very appropriately records God's response to the current situation of heresy in the Ekklesia by calling forth Overcomers. But it goes beyond that to show us the ultimate outcome of God's dealings with the Ekklesia, with the world, and with satan. It truly brings everything together into one and consummates everything.

But what about the man who was responsible for these writings? What does the Lord teach us about him?

John and His Gospel

John stands alone and apart. He did not write anything until he was the last one to write. Matthew, Mark, and Luke had already written their accounts of Christ. Each was written from a different perspective, but they essentially contain the same information.

Matthew emphasizes Christ as the Messiah and King, Mark introduces Him as the Suffering Servant, and Luke shows Him to be the Son of Man. Some of the same events and teachings are recorded in more than one of these Gospels, and some things are recorded in all three. There is some repetition and confirmation among them. All these years John wrote nothing. Perhaps he believed the record of Matthew, Mark, and Luke was sufficient. In any event, his time had not come.

As the Ekklesia increasingly came under the influence of Antichrist, both from within and from without, John wrote his Gospel long after the other three. If you read John's Gospel you will find that it is harmonious with Matthew, Mark, and Luke, but it is also quite apart from them. There is a profoundness there that is not present in the others. We are not suggesting one Gospel is more inspired than the others, we simply say that the Gospel of John has a certain fragrance not found anywhere else. This is because it was written for a specific purpose during a specific time, and the circumstances surrounding its writing are different from the circumstances surrounding the writing of the other three.

While Matthew describes Christ the King, Mark describes Christ the Suffering Servant, and Luke describes Christ the Son of Man, John describes Christ the Son of God. John specifically says his Gospel was written that we may know that Jesus is the Son of God and that we may have Life through His Name (Jn. 20:31).

It is interesting to note that the heavenly beasts John saw before the throne seem to represent the four gospels (Rev. 4:7). The first was like a lion, representing the King, or the Gospel of Matthew. The second was like a calf, or oxen, representing the Servant, for the oxen is a beast of burden. This represents the Gospel of Mark. The third has the face of a man, and this is representative of the Son of Man, the theme of the Gospel of Luke. The fourth is like a flying eagle, representing the Son of God, who is exalted and seated in the heavenly places where only the eagles may soar. This seems to characterize the Gospel of John. Perhaps John discerned the need for adding the fourth Gospel when he received this heavenly revelation.

What makes John's Gospel unique, and why does he come forth near the end of his life and provide it for the Ekklesia? For one thing, it goes back further into history than the other Gospels. Because Matthew demonstrates Christ as King and Messiah, he begins with Abraham and traces the line through King David. Mark shows the Suffering Servant who has no genealogy or line to speak of, so he simply begins with John the Baptist and records no genealogy at all. Luke, desiring to show forth Christ as the Son of Man, rightly traces the ancestry of Jesus all the way back to Adam. "Son of Man" would be translated, "Bar-Adam," the son of Adam, and since Christ is alternatively known as the Second Adam and the Last Adam, this is to be expected from Luke.

But John goes back even further: "In the beginning was the Word. The Word was with God, and the Word was God... the Word was made flesh and dwelt among us" (Jn. 1:1,2,14 ff). Thus, John presents Christ as the preexistent and preeminent Son of God.

John's Gospel is particularly unique because it deals with internal and eternal truths more so than external things. A few miracles are recorded insofar as they represent some overriding truth and revelation into the very essence of Christ; however, John wants us to see the spiritual reality of things, not the outward particulars. He deals with principles, not just facts.

For instance, the raising of Lazarus from the dead is related in order to demonstrate that Christ is Resurrection and Life to all who believe into Him. It is included not just to show that Christ can raise the dead, but that He Himself *is* Resurrection and Life. In the healing of a man born blind, the miracle is included to demonstrate that Christ is the Light which is come into the world, Who is sent to make the blind see and to make the ones who think they see, blind. John goes beyond the miracle of the bread and fish and provides us with a lengthy discourse that demonstrates the significance of the miracle: Christ Himself is the Bread that came down from heaven. So all the miracles are presented in such a way as to give us insight into the Person of Jesus Christ, and not just miracles as being something in and of themselves. John wishes to emphasize the *prophetic significance* of these miracles as revelations of Christ.

So we see in John's gospel more than just the relating of facts and anecdotal evidences. Grand, eternal, invisible truths are presented. Even so, we note how simply and succinctly these truths are presented.

Even a newborn Christian can read, understand, and benefit from John's Gospel, and we usually suggest that new believers, beginning a study of the New Testament, start with this book first. It touches upon things pertaining to Life, Love, Light, Water, Bread, One Flock, One Shepherd, the Way, the Truth, and more. Yet we do not touch these "things" – we touch a Man. Hallelujah!

Moreover, John's gospel is unique in that the majority of material presented is not found anywhere else. We have already mentioned how John goes all the way back to the beginning, to the preexistent Christ. This is exclusive to the Gospel of John. We also have the conversation with Nicodemus, the woman at the well, the woman caught in adultery, the resurrection of Lazarus, the detailed teaching of the Vine and Branches, the work of the Comforter, and the restoration of Peter. These are but a few examples of material that is unique to the Gospel of John.

The First Letter of John

When we come to John's letters we find the same fragrance within them as we do within his Gospel. If Paul is the teacher, the explainer, and the detailer, then John is the one who summarizes everything Paul ever said about Christ into one place: "He that has the Son has Life, and He that has not the Son of God has not Life" (1 Jn. 5:12). It just cannot be expressed more plainly or simply. John never mentions anything about head coverings, or spiritual gifts, or the qualifications of an elder. Concerning husbands and wives, parents and children, masters and slaves, widows and orphans, he says nothing; he ties everything up into one succulent truth: "Love one another."

All the details have been covered by Paul already. John's work is not to set the Ekklesia in order, but *to restore the Testimony of Jesus to the Ekklesia.* If the Ekklesia does not bear the Testimony then the matters of head covering, speaking in tongues, and eldership become moot points. In other words, if the Light goes out, then it does not matter if everything else is done decently and in order. We will simply be having "church" in the dark. If the Testimony of Jesus is lost then the meeting together, the Lord's Supper, the establishing of new fellowships, the exercise of spiritual gifts, the ministry to the poor – all that pertains to the Ekklesia becomes meaningless and dead.

As a wise master builder, Paul is building upon the foundation of Christ and concerns himself with everything from the building materials, to the color of the carpet and the fixtures on the wall (figuratively speaking). From Paul we learn all about this Ekklesia that Jesus is building. Once that is established, John comes to remind us why the spiritual building is built in the first place and Who the Owner is. In other words, John is calling us back to the *Testimony of Jesus* in order to recover God's original thought and purpose for the Ekklesia.

So in his first letter, John speaks with great liberty and sets forth the foundational truths in a way that sums up everything. As he nears the end of his life he sees the Ekklesia in a fallen position and endeavors to bring it back to an internal reality that transcends the outward structure. Of course he knows he is the last of the original twelve apostles. Peter, Paul, James... all of them have been killed. As John looked around at the condition of the Ekklesia it must have been a frightening thing to realize that he was the last of the Twelve and he was about to go too. But the Lord gives him an understanding and moves upon John to tell us that the Anointing Who abides in us will lead us into all truth, even if there are no apostles left to teach us.

Even if the outward structure fails (as it most certainly has, and did), the inward reality will see us through. John's words here are remarkably similar to the words of the Lord Jesus, who promised that even though He was leaving them, the Spirit would come and teach them everything. It is as though John senses the end is near and in one final act casts the care of the Ekklesia back upon the Spirit to look after his "little children."

The Second Letter of John

In the second letter of John there does not seem to be as much liberty. The audience seems to have shrunk considerably, and the letter is much shorter. In his first letter, he addresses everyone: fathers, young men, and little children. But now John rejoices that he "found [some] of your children" were holding to the truth (2

Jn. 4). Some of the children remained in the Truth; obviously, some did not. The letter warns against Antichrist and pleads with them not to receive anyone who does not bring the doctrine of Christ. What is the doctrine of Christ? It is that which has been revealed thus far concerning Jesus as the Christ of God and the Sum of All Things: *the Testimony of Jesus*.

The Third Letter of John

In the third letter of John there is even more trouble: for now the audience has been reduced to a single individual, Gaius, who alone abides in the Truth. Now, we do not mean to suggest that everyone has left the faith but Gaius, but we are suggesting that the three letters of John are arranged and written in a way that is representative of the decline of the Whole. John addresses everyone, then a few of the children, then one man. This is a decline. John is being shut up and shut out. For now we see that John himself is being rejected by Diotrephes. It is not merely the doctrine of Christ that is in dispute, but John himself is being called into question. Certainly some of the Ekklesia still received John, but then there are some who did not. The Ekklesia has come to a low place indeed, and we know that in at least one assembly, neither John nor his letters were allowed (3 Jn. 9).

The Fourth Letter of John (The Book of Revelation)

At some point prior to the decease of John, the letter of Jude was written to put the Ekklesia into remembrance of certain things that they ought to know, but had forgotten. There is little praise to be found here, although it holds out the promise that Christ can keep them from falling and will preserve them. Jude has to remind them of the teachings of the apostles. Most scholars believe that at the time of this writing the original apostles had already been martyred, the elderly John being the one exception.

So when the rest of the apostles had been martyred and the Ekklesia had fallen into a state of decline, John alone remained as the "last" apostle. God extended his years and kept him from martyrdom. Indeed, he was the only apostle to die a natural death. All the other apostles were executed. We ought to pay attention to that, because God is causing John to stand out from the other apostles. We see him in great contrast to the rest. What is God desiring us to see here?

The Lord wants us to see that John is an Overcomer. Though they boil him in oil, yet he has overcome death. Though they have exiled him to an island he overcomes, as this prepares him for his greatest contribution to the Ekklesia: his final letter to the Ekklesia, known as *The Book of Revelation*.

Without the Book of Revelation neither the New Testament nor the entire Bible can be brought to a fitting conclusion. Without it we are left to wonder how God will deal with the problem of Antichrist in the world and apostasy in the Ekklesia. God preserved John so that we may know the end of all things, and that we may know that there is a duty for us to fulfill and a role for us to play in the conclusion of all things.

Revelation and Testimony: Paul vs. John

To further illustrate the importance of Testimony, we should observe a key difference between Paul and John. Paul stressed the *Revelation of Christ*, whereas John emphasized the *Testimony of Jesus*. Paul represents Revelation, and John represents Testimony. Let us compare the two and see how they are different, yet connected.

- Revelation is from God to the Ekklesia, while Testimony is from the Ekklesia to the world.

- Revelation is an inward work, whereas Testimony is an outward witness.

- Revelation is the foundation upon which the Ekklesia is built, whereas the Testimony is the purpose for the building.

- Revelation is knowing, Testimony is showing.

- Revelation is the unveiling of Truth to the individual, Testimony is the unveiling of Truth to others.

- Revelation is seeing, Testimony is declaring what we have seen.

So while Paul is primarily concerned with helping all saints to come to the *epignosis* (full-knowledge) of Christ, John is primarily concerned with calling forth those who are to walk in the *epignosis* that they have received already. Paul is bringing forth mysteries in Christ that are now revealed and made apparent, while John is telling us to remember, know, and live according to the Truth that has already been revealed to us – to return to the foundation once laid. Thus, we see that Revelation is followed by Testimony. In a court of law, if we attempt to give testimony about something we have not seen or heard firsthand, that testimony is considered hearsay and is inadmissible. Spiritually speaking the same holds true. We cannot testify to what we have seen and heard if we have not, in fact, seen or heard anything to begin with.

Here is the Remnant Principle from Daniel, repeated again in the Book of Revelation. When the Ekklesia as a whole fails to maintain the Testimony of Jesus, God selects Overcomers, taking a few parts to represent the Whole. God has had His Overcomers in every season and age of the Ekklesia. Because of their ministry and service, the Kingdom of God is advancing. It is not losing ground at all. We must understand that God never moves backward in relation to Christ, even when circumstances seem to indicate huge reversals and detours from God's Ultimate Will. Since the foundation of the world He has moved steadily and patiently *forward*.

In the end, at the time of greatest darkness, God reveals His Son as King of Kings and Lord of Lords, Alpha and Omega, First and Last, Beginning and End, The One Who Overcame. He selects seven groups of believers to address and expresses His intention to carry out His Will and bring forth His Kingdom through Overcomers. John's ministry is that of *releasing and equipping Overcomers*. Where Peter casts the nets as a fisher of men to bring people into the Ekklesia, John is mending the nets after they have been torn (Mk. 1:19).

John is typical of all Overcomers. Notice that his greatest contribution to the Ekklesia is in his old age and at a time of spiritual darkness. Although we know that he worked diligently among the Ekklesia in Asia Minor as a pastor, teacher, and elder, Scripture holds him in relative obscurity until the time of the end. Then, like a treasured vessel, after everything is broken down and falling apart, John is brought out of insignificance and is given the crucial work of restoring the Testimony of Jesus to the Ekklesia, that the ultimate plan and purpose of God may be fulfilled. Since John is an Overcomer, God sends out the call for Overcomers through John. John is symbolic of all Overcomers, and he is the instrument through which God raises up Overcomers.

I can relate to John. I know many of us feel as if we are alone, in exile, in a wilderness. Gradually we feel we are being shut up and shut out by others who have not seen what we have seen. It is right there, in the desert place, in the place of exile, in the place of banishment, in the place of dryness, in the place of darkness, that Christ is revealed to us. This ought to encourage us no matter what our situation is.

"This is the Testimony"

We have previously seen that the Testimony of Jesus inspires the prophetic word (Rev. 19:10). We have defined this generally as "the truth concerning Jesus." What exactly is *the testimony of Jesus*?

John gives us a precise definition, but it requires the use of a concordance to unlock the meaning. If you simply look up the word "testimony" you only find a few relevant verses. For some inexplicable reason, the translators who gave us the King James Version decided on several occasions to translate a single Greek word into multiple English words. This means we have to take an extra step in our study, but it is not too difficult.

If we look up the word testimony we find it is a translation of the Greek word *martyria*. This is where we get our English word "martyr" from. If we trace all New Testament occurrences of the Greek word *martyria* we see that it appears 38 times and is translated four different ways in the King James Version: *witness* (15 times); *testimony* (14 times); *record* (7 times); and *report* (2 times).

So with this bit of detective work out of the way, we can now correctly determine exactly what John meant by *the Testimony of Jesus*. He explains it in his first letter:

> "This is he that came by water and blood, even Jesus Christ; not by water only, but by water and blood. And it is the Spirit that beareth witness (*martyria*), because the Spirit is truth. For there are three that bear record (*martyria*) in heaven, the Father, the Word, and the Holy Ghost: and these three are one. And there are three that bear witness (*martyria*) in earth, the Spirit, and the water, and the blood: and these three agree in one. If we receive the witness (*martyria*) of men, the witness (*martyria*) of God is greater: for this is the witness (*martyria*) of God which he hath testified (*martyreō*) of his Son. He that believeth on the Son of God hath the witness (*martyria*) in himself: he that believeth not God hath made him a liar; because he believeth not the record (*martyria*) that God gave (*martyreō*, testified) of his Son. And this is the record (*martyria*), that God hath given to us eternal life, and this life is in his Son. He that hath the Son hath life; and he that hath not the Son of God hath not life" (1 Jn. 5:6-12).

In this case we see the translators decided to use three different English words (*witness*, *record*, and *testify*) for the exact same Greek word (*martyria*), all in a single passage. Do you see how this makes it difficult to interpret?

How should it be translated? We can start by assigning the same English word (*testimony*) wherever the one Greek word (*martyria*) appears. If *martyria* is in the verb form (*martyreō*) then we will assign it a single English verb form (*testify*). That way we can compare apples to apples, oranges to oranges, and make the necessary connections. Here is what we have now:

> "It is the Spirit that *testifies*, because the Spirit is truth. For there are three that *testify* in heaven, the Father, the Word, and the Holy Ghost: and these three are one. And there are three that *testify* in earth, the Spirit, and the water, and the blood: and these three agree in one."

Isn't this easier to understand? Let us keep reading:

> "If we receive the *testimony* of men, the *testimony* of God is greater: for this is the *testimony* of God which He hath *testified* of His Son. He that believeth on the Son of God hath the *testimony* in himself: he that believeth not God hath made Him a liar; because he believeth not the *testimony* that God *testified* of His Son."

And now comes the answer to the big question: what is the testimony of Jesus?

> "**And this is the *testimony***, that God hath given to us eternal life, and this life is in His Son. He that hath the Son hath life; and he that hath not the Son of God hath not life."

"*This is the testimony.*" So, later when John writes that "*the testimony (martyria) of Jesus is the essence of prophecy,*" we know what the Testimony is: the Life is in the Son. If you have the Son, you have the Life; if you don't have the Son, you don't have the Life.

What does *that* mean? It means that *all are saved in Jesus and none are saved outside of Him*. It perfectly supports the very words of Jesus, also recorded by John: "I am the Way, the Truth, and the Life: no one comes to the Father except by Me" (Jn. 14:6). This statement points to the revelation of the Eternal Purpose of God: that in all things Christ must have the preeminence. God has set the Son in the ultimate place of authority, establishing that all are saved in Him and none are saved without Him.

The Testimony of Jesus Rejected

That simple statement – all are saved in Jesus, none are saved without Him - stands in stark contrast to the way of the world, the liberal culture, and the spirit of religion. How dare anybody suggest that *Jesus* is the only way to the Father! This is offensive to the Jew, the Muslim, the Buddhist, the Hindu, the Sikh, the Wiccan, the atheist, and every other stream of belief, including some so-called Christians. We are instead told that there are many paths to God, many expressions of faith. We have been told that all people of faith worship the same God, whether you call Him (or Her) God, Jehovah, Allah, The Universal Spirit, or some other name. We have been told that each path is valid for the person who happens to be traveling it, and that all roads lead to the same place. We have been told that only narrow-minded bigots and religious fanatics suggest that *their* way is the only correct way. Besides, what gives one group of people the right to judge another about what is right or wrong? In the name of love, harmony, ecumenicalism and universal brotherhood, we must (so they say) embrace all people and all beliefs. Diversity, tolerance, and unquestioned acceptance are the order of the day.

We are rapidly heading toward a time when the governments of this world will be forced to regulate and censor "religious speech" as the only solution to world peace. They will (correctly) determine that religion is the source of most of the world's wars and deaths from war. They will then move decisively to silence, punish, and eliminate anyone who disturbs the peace with "hate speech," which they will define as anything that appears to offend someone else's beliefs or religious practices. This will not violate the conscience of most of the world's religions, who will be allowed to practice their faith however they please, so long as they do not infringe upon the religious faith of others. But for the ones who bear *the Testimony of Jesus* – that all are saved in Him, and none are saved apart from Him – this will lead to widespread, universal persecution and death. Eventually, politics and religion will merge into a single entity that destroys all that oppose it.

This is not some wild conspiracy theory; it is precisely what the Book of Revelation describes.

> "When He opened the fifth seal, I saw under the altar the souls of those who had been slain for the word of God and for the testimony (*martyria*) which they held" (Rev. 6:9).

> "When they finish their testimony (*martyria*), the beast that ascends out of the bottomless pit will make war against them, overcome them, and kill them" (Rev. 11:7).

> "And they overcame him by the blood of the Lamb and by the word of their testimony (*martyria*), and they did not love their lives to the death" (Rev. 12:11).

> "And the dragon was enraged with the woman, and he went to make war with the rest of her offspring, who keep the commandments of God and have the testimony (*martyria*) of Jesus Christ" (Rev. 12:17).

> "I saw the souls of them that were beheaded for the witness (*martyria*) of Jesus, and for the word of God" (Rev. 20:4).

Amateurs of Bible prophecy, who would immediately dismiss these verses as being only applicable to some future period of time that does not affect them, are badly misinformed. All the established institutions of this world – government, religion, education, banking, commerce, military, media, and entertainment – are today becoming united under a single goal. There is a great darkness that directs and coordinates their efforts towards a specific end. Do they even realize what they are doing? Probably not, but whether they realize it or not, the powerful men and women in the institutions of this world are mere pawns being moved across the board toward a goal that they cannot even fathom.

Of all people, those who bear *the Testimony of Jesus* are singled out. For what reason? There is a spiritual wickedness that works within the world's institutions and systems and seeks to destroy the Testimony of Jesus. We know it as the Dragon, the Serpent, the Beast, Satan. But all these identities can be summed up into a single persona: it is *the spirit of Antichrist* – that evil force that stands *against* and *in the place of* Christ; and therefore, *against* and *in the place of* the Testimony of Jesus. This is the spirit behind the desire to unite the governments of this world into a single entity and exert political and religious control over the entire population of the world. And according to Scripture, God will permit it to succeed for a period of time immediately preceding the literal, visible return of Jesus Christ to personally govern the nations of this earth and prevent them from destroying the whole population of the world (Mt. 24:22). The process is well underway.

The world rejects the Testimony of Jesus. The spirit of Antichrist is determined to destroy the Testimony of Jesus. Yet this Testimony of Jesus – that He is the only Way to the Father – is the foundation of Christian belief and the essence of all prophetic revelation and utterance. Any attempt to minimize this or to suggest that all other paths to God are equally valid violates this Testimony. This Testimony puts the claims of Christ at variance with every other religious path. It is the cornerstone of our faith, the foundation of all we believe – and the only hope for the salvation of mankind. No wonder the adversary fights against it.

Chapter Fourteen

The Prophetic Mandate

"I have made you a watchman for the house of Israel; therefore you shall hear a word from My mouth and warn them for Me" (Eze. 33:7).

A *mandate* is an authoritative instruction or command. It comes from a Latin word that means, "to give into someone's hand," meaning that they have an authority and responsibility to perform a particular task. From this word *mandate* comes the word *mandatory*, which means to make something a requirement, a non-negotiable essential. In Old Testament times, the watchman on the city wall had a *mandate* to warn of any dangers that approached. This was his only duty. To carry it out, staying awake and alert was *mandatory*. If the watchman fell asleep and failed to warn the people, their blood would be on his hands.

Similarly, the Lord has provided a *prophetic mandate* to those men and women who are called to the prophetic ministry in our time. This age is unique in the sense that it is considered "the dispensation of the fullness of the times," or, "the last days." The prophetic mandate today is not to keep watch over a city, but to keep watch over the Ekklesia (a "heavenly city" if you will) to ensure that the Eternal Purpose of God in Christ is fulfilled.

Scripture acknowledges that while everything is *technically* under the feet of Christ today (since Jesus is Lord), the fact remains that "we do not yet see all things put under Him" (Heb. 2:8). The word *yet* indicates that one day we *will* see all things put under Him. In the meantime, most of us just wait for the fulfillment of that Eternal Purpose.

But the prophetic person does not passively *wait* for anything. The prophet agonizes over the condition of the world, wrestles with God, sees His Purpose, declares it to others, and rises up daily to pray, fast, and fight to ensure that the Purpose is fulfilled. The prophet watches over the Ekklesia, helps it grow, keeps it from drifting off course, weeps when it does, and endeavors to set it right again. The prophet discerns the spiritual enemy working behind the scenes, warns of its dangers, challenges it, and demands its submission to the preeminence of Christ. The prophet observes the ebb and flow of things in the world and evaluates what impact this could have on the Ekklesia and the Purpose of God: are things moving *towards* God's Purpose or *away* from it? The prophet seeks wisdom and understanding and works in harmony with the Holy Spirit to help, encourage, strengthen, warn, and prepare the Ekklesia for what lies ahead. One need only read the Book of Daniel to find Scriptural support of the life I have just described.

To see and hear clearly, the prophet has to remain "above the fray." To climb down from the wall and become immersed in the minutia and trivia of the day is to invite disaster: "I sent messengers to them, saying, 'I am doing a great work, so that I cannot come down. Why should the work cease while I leave it and go down to you?'" (Neh. 6:3). The prophetic mandate requires the prophet to be on duty, before the Lord, watching and waiting at all times: day and night, holidays and weekends, in every season, in every place, and in every condition. This is not usually possible outwardly; but inwardly, it is an indispensable necessity.

Threat Assessment: Opposition to the Testimony of Jesus in Our Age

A fighter pilot must always be alert to the threats and intentions of enemy forces as well as the status of his own aircraft. When a pilot gets lost, becomes disoriented, or is surprised by something he should have been prepared for, he is said to have lost "situational awareness."

Most Christians in western society are living in a grand delusion. Too many assume that western civilization and Christianity will just continue on as it always has. They are (for the most part) completely unaware and unconcerned about preserving the Testimony of Jesus or handing down a Christ-Centered Faith to the next generation. They have completely lost their "situational awareness."

Meanwhile, the scale and sophistication of attacks against the Testimony of Jesus have certainly increased over the last 2,000 years. Jesus said that the days preceding His return would be "as in the days of Noah" (Mt. 24:37). Concerning those days, Scripture records:

> "The Lord saw that the wickedness of man was great in the earth, and that every intent of the thoughts of his heart was only evil continually... The earth also was corrupt before God, and the earth was filled with violence." (Gen. 6:5,11).

Any historian or statistician can confirm that the world is corrupt and getting worse. Rather than restate the obvious, let us look more deeply and identify the major enemies that threaten the Testimony of Jesus and seek to hinder the continuity of a Christ-Centered Faith in our day.

1. *Compromise of the Institutional Church.* Without question, the Institutional Church ("Churchianity") has replaced the authentic belief and practice of the New Testament Ekklesia. It has emerged as the single greatest hindrance to the spiritual growth and maturity of the Ekklesia. As a result of a sovereign move of God, many have been led to quit Churchianity and seek alternative means of fellowship with others. This has created a host of new problems as well as many fresh opportunities. Meanwhile, in an effort to remain relevant and cling to its dwindling power, the Institutional Church has adapted itself to whatever society demands, becoming

increasingly carnal and compromised in the process. What Light it may have enjoyed has long ago been extinguished. God permits it to remain for a season, but it is little more than a whitewashed tomb full of dead men's bones – both figuratively and literally.

2. *Moral Decay of Society.* The last fifty years in particular have witnessed a remarkable and speedy slide towards new depths of depravity and debauchery. We could go down the list: murder and violence, pornography, rape, adultery, homosexuality, drug and alcohol abuse, child abuse, and perversions too vile to put into print are increasingly tolerated, then accepted, then legalized. Take for example the homosexual agenda. For thousands of years, the judgment of God on Sodom and Gomorrah was figuratively burned into the collective conscience of mankind. Homosexuality was usually punished if discovered. Laws against sodomy were on the books for many centuries. Today, homosexuality is seen as acceptable, trendy, cool, progressive, and normal. Gay politicians and entertainers are applauded and lifted up as idols and examples to follow. The conventional definition of marriage is up for debate and gay marriage is legal in many nations and in many states. The Institutional Church ordains gay ministers and either

performs gay marriages (when legal) or blesses gay unions. Liberal theologians (and quite a few ignorant "believers") condemn those who are not more open-minded and accepting of same-sex relationships; which to them means ignoring sexual sin and explaining away the clear teaching of Scripture. It is no longer enough to love the sinner and hate his sin; we must now love the sinner and accept his sin. Now anyone critical of homosexuals opens themselves up to be arrested and prosecuted for "hate crimes." This is just one example of how society always moves towards an "anything goes" mentality if there is no basic moral standard that we can all agree on and be submitted to. "You shall not at all do as we are doing here today—every man doing whatever is right in his own eyes" (Deut. 12:8).

3. *Government Overreach.* There is a reason why Paul told Timothy to "pray for kings and for all who are in authority." It was not just so that kings and presidents could "be saved" or because it is the "Christian thing to do" to pray for our political leaders. The reason was: "so we can live a quiet, peaceful life in all godliness and honesty" (1 Tim. 2:2). Paul was telling Timothy to pray that the government will leave us alone. To the extent that the government leaves its citizens alone, to that

extent they can live quietly and in peace. History teaches that an intrusive, overreaching government taxes too much, spends too much, legislates too much, and kills too much. The general trend of the world is towards liberal, intrusive government that taxes and regulates every aspect of life. It then becomes all that much easier for government to insert itself into matters of faith: abortion, contraception, homosexuality, marriage, and what is considered acceptable and unacceptable religious speech and practices. By the time the people realize that they have given the government too much power, it is too late for them change it. The general trend of the governments of this world show that we are fast approaching the one-world government predicted by Scripture.

4. *Radical Islam and Islamic Jihadists.* Experts confirm that Islam is a religious as well as a political force with the sufficient means, motivation, and ability to destroy western society. A thorough explanation of radical Islam is well beyond the scope of this book. It is enough for me to simply point out that there is a significant population in the world today that wishes to conquer the whole world for Islam, impose Sharia (Islamic) Law on all people, and kill anyone who does not convert to Islam. Pick any country where Islam is the

dominating power and judge the fruit for yourself. One of the tenets of Islam is that God has no Son. Thus, Islam is directly opposed to the Testimony of Jesus and cannot be compatible with a Christ-Centered Faith. Yet, we see leaders in the Institutional Church using every means possible to join together with Muslim leaders in the name of "brotherhood." This shows unbelievable ignorance. Consider this: Saudi Arabia (an Islamic nation) uses public beheading as punishment for murder, rape, drug trafficking, sodomy, armed robbery, and, of course, those who attempt to convert away from the Muslim religion. The Taliban also practices this method of execution, as do Muslim terrorists. Scripture tells us that the end-time souls who are martyred for the Testimony of Jesus are "beheaded" (Rev. 20:4). Could this help us to identify the religious and political power that fights against those who bear the Testimony of Jesus in the Book of Revelation? We have already seen what happens around the world when someone "insults Islam." Soon, criticizing Islam or its Prophet will be classified as "hate speech." He who has an ear, let him hear.

5. *Worn out saints.* "[The Antichrist] shall speak great words against the most High, and shall

wear out the saints of the most High" (Dan. 7:25). By and large, the saints are already worn down and worn out. The majority of Christians are thoroughly unprepared for spiritual conflict and are not even thinking about spiritual war. The combined weight of things we face in these times threatens the strength and vitality of God's people. Believers are under constant spiritual, mental, emotional, physical, and financial attack, and with precious little energy to spare, we typically waste it fighting one another over things that are irrelevant. We have the opportunity to live as Overcomers, to demonstrate the preeminence of Christ over all things, and to walk in victory – even in the midst of perilous times such as these. But the saints, for the most part, are simply too tired, too self-absorbed with their own problems, and too distracted by the cares of this world to give much effort or concern to anyone or anything else. Jesus said that "sin will be rampant everywhere, and the love of many will grow cold" (Mt. 24:12, NLT). When people are busy and stressed out and just trying to make it from one day to the next, there isn't much time, money, or energy left to devote to Kingdom purposes.

6. *Lack of spiritual leadership.* Paul observed that "though you might have ten thousand

instructors in Christ, yet you do not have many fathers" (1 Cor. 4:15). If this was true in Paul's day, it is all the more true in our day. We not only lack true spiritual fathers – we lack true apostles and prophets; we lack true evangelists, pastors and teachers; we lack true *elder* brothers and sisters in Christ who are ready, able, and willing to lay down their lives in service to the Ekklesia. The wounds of religion run deep, and many who have survived it have sworn off leadership as unneeded and unnecessary. Meanwhile, the Ekklesia suffers from spiritual infancy and a chronic failure to grow up. Most have never experienced true, godly, Christ-centered spiritual leadership; all they have known is the suffering, abuse, and neglect they experienced at the hands of hirelings employed by the Institutional Church.

The Way Forward

The purpose for identifying threats to our Testimony is not to cause us to lose hope, but to stir us to action. What I have described thus far is nothing new or surprising. It is all contained within the record of Scripture. But in spite of all this, the Book of Revelation records that God's people are active participants in the Last Days. Many are killed for their faith, true; but they are faithful to the Testimony of Jesus. They are Overcomers, not Defeatists. They resist Antichrist.

They refuse the Mark. They wage spiritual war and hold steadfast until the end. "The people who know their God shall be strong, and carry out great exploits" (Dan. 11:32).

Even in the early days of the Ekklesia, Paul had already seen by the Spirit that the Last Days would be perilous and difficult. He might have shrugged his shoulders and accepted the inevitable; but he did not do so. Instead, in his final letter to Timothy, on the eve of his own death, Paul gave this specific instruction: "Teach these things to faithful people who can teach others" (2 Tim. 2:2).

The fact that Paul was concerned for the *handing down* of a Christ-Centered Faith is very significant. **If Christ-centered teaching is not preserved and handed down to the next generation, it will be lost in the milieu of liberalism, atheism, Churchianity, and false religions.** It is very nearly lost already. The Institutional Church is impotent, ineffective, and compromised beyond repair. We must do what the Institutional Church has failed to do: we must teach *these things* to faithful people who can teach others to ensure the continuity of the Testimony of Jesus until He returns.

Each generation believes that they are the "last" generation, but no one knows for sure when the end will come. Where would you and I be if some previous generation determined that the end was near and decided *not* to preserve a Christ-Centered Faith hand down to us? What if we decide there is nothing more we can do but take care of ourselves and wait for the end to come; what will become of the next generation? Are we willing to be known as the first and only generation that failed to hand down the Testimony of Jesus? Will we be responsible for the death of Christianity?

Some may say that God will never let His Testimony falter, that He will always preserve the message of Christ, and taking so much care and concern is unnecessary. I think this attitude reflects the lazy, self-centered nature of a Laodicean. Of course God can, in His infinite power, do whatever He wishes and does not need me or you or anyone to accomplish His Purpose. Nevertheless, we see in the Book of Revelation that when the majority of God's people are backslidden, lazy, lukewarm, and indifferent, God uses Overcomers to carry out His Purpose.

A tremendous door is open. The growing dissatisfaction and disillusionment with the Institutional Church provides the Ekklesia with a once-in-a-lifetime opportunity to bring these hurting, wounded people into a genuine relationship with Christ that is not based on church membership. Not to mention the fact that, as times get tougher and traditional institutions collapse, the Ekklesia must be ready to provide alternative communities of social and spiritual support (for example, home groups) to encourage, help, and care for their members and for those who are seeking truth. The Harvest is indeed plentiful – but are we prepared for it?

Foundations of Christ-Centered Faith

> "If the foundations are destroyed, what can the righteous do?" (Ps. 11:3).

Just 400 years ago it was commonly accepted that everything in the universe, including the sun, moon and stars, all revolved around a stationary Earth. Not only did this seem obvious to those who lived on Earth, it seemed to be supported by Scripture.

So when the astronomer Galileo began to spread the idea of the earth and everything else revolving around a stationary sun, he attracted the ire of the Roman Catholic Church. Galileo provided a solid scientific basis for his ideas, and tried to show that his theories did not contradict Scripture at all. Nevertheless, Galileo was branded a heretic, forced to recant, and obliged to live the rest of his life as a prisoner in his own home. Today we know that the Roman Catholic Church was wrong, and Galileo was correct.

In a similar way, the Christian Religion has, for over 1700 years, successfully convinced millions of people to adopt a *Church-Centered Faith*. Scriptures are used to justify a view of the spiritual universe that is erroneous. It is a line of thinking in which everyone and everything connected with God is supposed to revolve around the Church: build it, support it, attend it, and invite people to join it. Christ, mistakenly credited with having founded this Church, is in their eyes obliged to protect, defend, love, honor, cherish, bless, and provide for it. Those who challenge this view are likewise seen as rebellious heretics.

The truth is that God *never* called us to a Church-Centered Faith. From the beginning, God has called followers of Jesus to a *Christ-Centered Faith*: a way of living that revolves around Christ having the central, preeminent, and most important place in a person's heart. The Assembly of Called-Out Persons (the Ekklesia) was to be both a spiritual and a practical community of Christ-followers who had entered into a new covenant with God and with one another: to value, believe, teach, practice, and experience a Christ-Centered Faith.

That is simply another way of saying that the belief and practice of the New Testament was based upon, and centered around, a relationship with a Person. The focus was not on the systematic theology of a new religious group, nor was it the particular nuance of doctrine from a breakaway splinter group within Judaism. New Testament belief and practice was unique in that it was centered upon a Man Who lived, died, came back to life again, and would now rule in the hearts of men and women until He returned. You could say that in the New Testament universe, God clearly established that everything was to revolve around the SON.

If the foundations are destroyed, what can the righteous do? I believe the answer, as it pertains to the Ekklesia, is to go back to the One Foundation that cannot be destroyed: Christ Jesus the Lord. "For no other foundation can anyone lay than that which is laid, which is Jesus Christ" (1 Cor. 3:11). This Foundation is strong and secure.

We must tear down the flimsy structures we have built and rebuild upon the firm foundation of Christ. I offer the following Four Pillars as a basis upon which the Ekklesia can re-establish itself in the current age and ensure the continuity of an authentic, Biblical, Christ-Centered Faith for this generation and for however many will follow.

1. *The Testimony of Jesus.* The preeminence of Christ must be the cornerstone of all our belief and practice. Remember, this Testimony declares that "all are saved in Him, none are saved apart from Him." This Testimony inspires all prophetic utterance. This Testimony is our lamp, and if the lamp is extinguished, the Ekklesia ceases to exist (Rev. 2:5). We cannot dilute, distort, or disfigure this Testimony for any reason. If we fail to discern and declare *the truth concerning Jesus* to the world around us, then we have utterly failed.

2. *Scriptural Integrity.* Before we seek new, exciting revelation we must master what has already been revealed. The Scriptures are necessary for the spiritual growth and spiritual discernment of the Ekklesia. The Written Word reveals the Living Word, and the Living Word reveals the Written Word: "Then Jesus took them through the writings of Moses and all the prophets, explaining from all the Scriptures the things concerning Himself" (Lk. 24:27, NLT). Since Jesus thought

Scriptural teaching was important for His disciples, we cannot afford to lightly dismiss it. We must know the Scriptures, obey them, and teach them to others.

3. *Intentional Fellowship.* The post-church landscape is a lot like the Dark Ages after the Roman Empire collapsed; with no institution to keep them in check, people ran wild. In the absence of the Institutional Church, the Ekklesia must provide safe places where people can learn about Jesus in a non-religious, non-traditional setting. Intentional Fellowship means that we gather together for a purpose: to reach *up* to God, to reach *in* to one another, and to reach *out* to the world around us. We must transcend the "meeting" mentality we inherited from the Institutional Church and begin to think in terms of an extended Family that nurtures long-term relationships and meets both spiritual and practical needs.

4. *Passing the Torch.* To successfully hand down a Christ-Centered Faith to the next generation, three things are needed. First, we must master the core teachings that constitute basic discipleship; those essential elements of the Faith that need to be passed down. Next, we must find and equip faithful people who know these essentials and will teach them to others. Finally, we must create opportunities for real discipleship

to take place within the faith community of the Ekklesia – a nurturing, safe place to be born-again, to be healed, to learn, to grow, and to go forth; a place where spiritual wisdom can be imparted.

Oh Ekklesia, House of Living Stones! Jesus wants you as a spiritual house, a holy priesthood, a habitation of the Most High God! Come, let us build together with Him, and secure the Testimony of Jesus in the earth until He returns! "Behold, I come quickly!" Amen – even so, come Lord Jesus.

Preserving a
Christ-Centered Faith

The School of Christ is here
to bring healing to those hurt by religion,
to provide for the spiritual growth and maturity of
all believers, and to ensure the continuity
of a Christ-Centered Faith.

To contact the author, obtain additional copies
of this book, or request a complete listing of
books, audio teachings, and other resources
available, please visit our website.

THE SCHOOL OF CHRIST

A — Ω

JOHN 3:30

TheSchoolOfChrist.Org

Printed in Dunstable, United Kingdom

68739935R00161